2

D1264206

No Rewind

ONLY ONE SHOT

Larry Bettag

WestBow·
PRESS
A DIVISION OF THOMAS NELSON
& ZONDERVAN

Copyright © 2014 Larry Bettag.

All rights reserved. No part of this book may be used or reproduced by
any means, graphic, electronic, or mechanical, including photocopying,
recording, taping or by any information storage retrieval system
without the written permission of the publisher except in the case
of brief quotations embodied in critical articles and reviews.

WestBow Press books may be ordered through booksellers or by contacting:

WestBow Press
A Division of Thomas Nelson & Zondervan
1663 Liberty Drive
Bloomington, IN 47403
www.westbowpress.com
1 (866) 928-1240

Because of the dynamic nature of the Internet, any web addresses or
links contained in this book may have changed since publication and
may no longer be valid. The views expressed in this work are solely those
of the author and do not necessarily reflect the views of the publisher,
and the publisher hereby disclaims any responsibility for them.

Any people depicted in stock imagery provided by Thinkstock are models,
and such images are being used for illustrative purposes only.
Certain stock imagery © Thinkstock.

ISBN: 978-1-4908-2674-5 (sc)
ISBN: 978-1-4908-2676-9 (hc)
ISBN: 978-1-4908-2675-2 (e)

Library of Congress Control Number: 2014903034

Printed in the United States of America.

WestBow Press rev. date: 03/11/2014

TESTIMONIALS

"The quality of our lives to a great extent is dependent on our perspective. In this book, Larry has done a masterful job of sharing stories of inspiration along with life truths in a way that is guaranteed to challenge your perspective. If you give this book a chance, I am confident it will positively impact the quality of your life!"

Daniel Harkavy, C.E.O. and Founder Building Champions

"Larry had me laughing, crying and simply moved with a powerful message that every person should read. Larry, thank you for sharing these incredible stories and life lessons that will impact each person who reads it. Once I started reading No Rewind, I couldn't put it down as I connected with every character, their challenges and their triumphs. Anyone wanting to be exceptional should read this book as Larry has a gift of writing with incredible persuasion and draws you in. Grab a cup of coffee or a glass of wine and happy reading!"

Casey Cunningham, C.E.O. and Founder of XINNIX Training Academy

"Once I started reading "No Rewind," I had a hard time putting it down. I don't say this about many books, but this is a must read. Few books have captured my heart and mind as quickly as "No Rewind." Get ready to look through your life with a new set of lenses."

Ronnie Doss, Founder and C.E.O. of Ronnie Doss Speaks

In a raw, unadulterated way, Larry gets to the heart of some life matters that actually matter. If you want a nice easy, cotton candy-like book that simply entertains and does no more, don't read this one. Instead, if you want a book that causes you to think in a way that can permanently impact your life then "No Rewind" is your next read. I am simply better for reading "No Rewind." I am grateful for you Larry, and the courage it took to get this out. I sure hope the world isn't too busy to read it.

Steve Scanlon, Founder and Chief Lizard at Rewire, Inc

"No Rewind" combines self-help, humor, struggle, and true courage. You'll walk away from this book with momentum to overcome your fears and make the most out of your life."

Rich Brennan, President and C.E.O. of Optimal Living Academy

Through "No Rewind" we learn from Larry's life that dreaming is right if married to action and planning. Dreaming is good. It's God-given and it's God empowered! Take the steps Larry lays out for you...your life will be changed...and God will smile.

Pastor Joe Barlow, Family Life Christian
Center & Joseph Barlow Ministries

INTRODUCTION

I was running some errands recently with my second oldest, Jake. We were talking about a couple we know who had broken into an abandoned home and had taken up residence there. They weren't married; they were professional partiers. They didn't work; they relied on government aid. They have a child, a fifth-grader who has been grossly neglected. The father and mother had been arrested a number of times.

Jake asked me how they got their money since neither worked. I told him they receive stipends from our government. He knew they drank a lot and were unemployed and had broken into the vacant house. They turned on the heat and electricity and still received monthly welfare or assistance checks.

Jake said, "No offense [not sure why, but the new slang always opens with "No offense"], Dad, but I played video games once for two hours straight and I felt bad about it. I can't imagine just doing what they do all the time. It must be pretty boring."

I told him God had a huge plan for that dad, mom, and child. I told him it was never too late to do what God wanted you to do and make your mark on the world. What that couple was doing was a shallow, empty pursuit of pleasure over meaning. Their actions were wrong and illegal. But I told Jake the cool thing was that God hadn't given up on them and that it wasn't too late for them to change and get their plans into action.

Everyone has a story to tell. God calls every person for a mission and promises them lots of adventures along the way. God doesn't want anyone as a bench warmer. There may be a learning curve, but he's called everyone to start the game. In *Give Your Speech, Change the World*, author Nick Morgan writes that if you're going to take the trouble to give a speech, you need to make it worthwhile. I'd go a step further and say if you're going to live a life, make an impact, you need to change the world as well.

I was an English major in college. Although it took me five years to get through college (too much partying), from what I remember, verb tenses are important. When I say, "You are called to be great now," the operative word is *now*. Being great is not about your past. It's not about your failures or missed opportunities or devastating tragedies or great successes. It's definitely not about tomorrow since tomorrow never comes. Your future is critical, and it begins today.

Many books try to get you to aspire to be a better you. While that's a worthy goal, life is way too short for you to settle for being only a better version of yourself. This book is meant for people who want to leave it all out on the field. "Go hard or go home" is the mantra of the superstar athlete. We have all been designed to be key players in the game of life.

Some people reading this book are already successful by the world's standards; they have cars, enjoy vacations, and are raising 2.3 kids. They are involved with churches, schools, neighborhoods, and charitable organizations. They are movers and shakers in whatever sphere they are in. But are they great?

Being great doesn't mean that you need to become a a nuclear physicist, brain surgeon, or pastor of a large church; it means doing something fulfilling that positively impacts the lives of others within the scope of the DNA given to you.

This book is designed to direct you to being the best version of yourself. Total fulfillment. Whether you are a librarian, custodian, housewife, or the president of a Fortune 500 company, this book is for you. Haven't you ever wanted to accomplish something over the top? Sure you have. We all have.

Coming with the "modernization" and "simplification" of life is the reality that most modern technological advancements have actually complicated life. I remember my dad having one of those three-pound cell phones. I thought it was so cool. He was a doctor, after all. Thirty years later, I have an iPhone, email, and text messaging, and I often work from a virtual office. None of these inventions has alleviated stress. Rather, they have put me closer to the stressors that intrude in my life. I'm accessible always, unless I do something about it. I have little time to achieve, create, grow, and serve because I need to respond to the incessant barrage of stimuli.

We think that by responding, we'll get caught up. I have some shocking news here: we never get caught up. It's impossible. By chasing that false promise, we lose our focus and end up passing on the big plans we were called to do.

You end up juggling the world's demands and shelving your true desires. It starts off as shelving a dream just for the time being until something of value happens in your life. The dream stays on hold until you graduate college, get married, have a baby, buy a new home, pay off your car, save for your kids' college fund, pay off that vacationandon and blah, blah, blah. And technology keeps advancing to make life easier?

Eventually, you end up settling for fun moments instead of living a fulfilling life. The most overwhelming truth is if you aren't working toward something that fulfills you from within, you're just filling yourself with moments. Empty moments. Time fillers. Moments to hide your emptiness or moments to create momentary pleasure. But when the pleasure ends, the same empty feeling returns. That truth is an absolute.

Your partner is now just a roommate. Maybe your marriage or relationship is okay, but it's not thriving as it once was. You knew you were going to be a great parent when you both decided it was time to have kids, but since then, your relationship with them has become more of a duty than an enjoyment. It will be better once you get done with the things you need to get through at work, you say. But your children's activities become chores for you, and even though they may not be able to psychologically discern your heart, they know you're not the parent you once were. You don't like the way you interact with your children. They can't explain it, but they know when you're engaged and when you're not. You're not as good to your children or spouse as you had wanted to be.

The good news is that changes now. Start visualizing your life as you had always wanted it to be. Do you remember those talks with your buddies growing up? "When I grow up, I'm going to _____." Those dreams you shelved need to be dusted off and put back in your pocket to carry with you everywhere.

Achieving your dreams won't be easy, but it will be fulfilling. I heard a great preacher once say that it's more fun making a million dollars than it is having it. Much work is involved in becoming great, but I assure you that if you can stir up your heart, you'll gain phenomenal inner peace and create a lot of excitement in becoming all you were designed to be. Looking back and seeing the muscles you have built along the way is most satisfying. Remember, muscle is built with resistance. What was Schwarzenegger's phrase? "No pain, no gain."

You were specifically designed by a greater being to do something great during your time on earth. Your efforts will enrich you as a person and change the world for the better while you're becoming who you were designed to be. Whether you believe in Christ, Allah, Buddha, the Great

Spirit, or whomever, your creator has designed you to change people's lives for the better and have a massive impact on your world.

Stress is a huge killer in the United States. Most diseases are caused by stress. You have ease or dis-ease. Living your life fully reduces your stress levels and puts your heart more at ease. Struggles will come, but if you are on the path you've been called to, those struggles will just be bumps set in front of you so you can grow, learn, and help you get to your true destination in life.

However, most of us have put this idea on a shelf because of the everyday stresses. The demands. The deadlines. We've shelved our dreams so we can deal with the day-to-day. This book isn't about time management, but it will teach you how to find, kindle, nurture, and commit to your passion. It will help you make your dreams happen no matter the obstacles. I've lived a very hectic life but have found a way to live in my passion, and I couldn't be more thrilled. I've had lots of ups and downs, but my vision drives me.

But this book isn't about me. Though I share my story, it's only to help you. This book is about you creating your own story.

HOW TO READ THIS BOOK

It's my hope that you'll find much value in this book. I read a lot of books. Some are fun. Some are encouraging. Some are thrilling. But there are a few I end up using as points of reference through life. I hope that by sharing with you the very easy way that I read, this book can become a point of reference for your life.

As I read, things jump out at me. If I'm going through a tough time and feel like quitting on a project but read something about "persistence," I'll underline that word and highlight the phrases that jump out and speak to me. In the front of the book, I write down "persistence" followed by the page numbers that refer to persistence. As other topics come up, I do the same. I don't write down every page that talks to my topics, just those that speak to me. Here's a sample of how my inside cover may look:

Faith: 24, 36, 77, 188, 202
Persistence: 88, 103, 176
Trials: 7, 72, 104, 105, 106
Failure: 2, 22, 98, 99, 100
Fear: 18, 19, 67, 92, 176

This allows me to avoid paging through the book to see the words that have spoken to me. If I'm going through a trial, I look at the inside cover for the word "trial" and go directly to the word or sections that spoke to me.

I also end up having multiple authors speak to me on topics important to me. I get the best of the best from each without having to search high and low for it. I encourage you to do this with this book.

A STRUGGLE TO ...

A challenge I sought
In this dark and ominous mountain
That silently stalks its prey.

The first day I set my speed fast.
My thighs burn with pulsating, ripping sensations
That strain to place the soil in the past.
No sooner do I begin than I crumble out of exhaustion.
I stop more and more.
Minutes lead only to mere steps that are small and painful.
Again, again, and again do I stop. I regain my stance
Only to fall down again out of frustrated pain.
The night nears as I rid my consciousness
Of pain with tears.

The few who survive are those who withstand the grueling
Forces of the environment. As lichen that clings to the
Granite rock of the alpine tundra, I remain. The elk on the
Mountainside struggles through the harsh winters that nature Challenges
it with.
Yet it survives.
The next mile will present me with the most excruciating
Pain yet encountered.
Like the elk, I too must fight or die.

My goal miraculously arrives. The eagle that fights for its territory
Never desires to reenact this, yet it would not trade this away as the
Crystal clear stream below is now its. The mountain, too, is now mine.
This was a challenge I struggled to even accept.
I will never climb this mountain again.
A new one that is more exciting and difficult
Lies ahead. This is a challenge I cannot
Deny myself of.

WENDY: VISION

Wendy (not her real name), the youngest of four sisters, was a beautiful, dynamic young woman with an effervescent personality. I was attracted to her when we met for our first session. I was an intern finishing my Master's Degree in clinical psychology when I had first met Wendy. She was my client. She was focused and well spoken. She dressed well and was quite attractive. Wendy maintained a good position at work. She was about twenty-one and dating a guy who loved her and treated her well. She had had an apartment since she was old enough to move out on her own. She seemed quite normal and balanced in most ways. To an outsider, it seemed as if she had the perfect life or at least a good life. Yet here she was coming to me for counseling. Something just wasn't right in her life.

Counseling isn't just for the broken. It is often used for mentally strong and healthy people to help them work through their issues. I wondered why Wendy was seeing me. Were there real problems or just minor issues she needed to settle to find a bit of peace?

Wendy told me she had anger issues. The anger would arise out of nowhere and turn into fits of rage against her seemingly perfect boyfriend. She admitted that her boyfriend was fair and kind to her and treated her with respect, but her anger was harsh and instantaneous. She couldn't explain why; he seemed perfect.

When a person comes to me with a perfect significant other, my radar goes up immediately. In this case, I wondered when the other shoe was going to drop concerning the boyfriend. It never did. He came and participated incounseling whenever she wanted. He basically was her rock and fortress. It became evident he was there to build her up, not tear her down.

Even after weeks of counseling, I couldn't understand what her issues were. Why the unexpected, unrelenting fits of anger? I wanted to know the real reason for her seeing me. After about three months of counseling, I was no closer to understanding the source of her anger. I kept waiting, listening, and subtly probing. Nothing. No leads. No cracks. Not a thing.

I finally had to tell Wendy that although I enjoyed her, she would be wasting her time and money if she continued to see me. I wouldn't be able to help someone who wouldn't let me in to help her. If there was nothing to fix, why bother? Maybe there was nothing more for her to share, or maybe it was too deep to discover. Maybe she just needed to take a chill pill and grow up. I suggested we get to the core issues or quit wasting our time and her money.

By then, we had more than established the proper rapport. The trust was there, so I felt comfortable giving Wendy that ultimatum. The threat cracked the iceberg; she began to open up. During that session, Wendy hemmed and hawed and fidgeted nervously. Something important was about to come out, and I was pleased. Wendy said she wanted to share something she'd been withholding. I anxiously waited. She took a deep breath, put her face in her hands, and began to cry. She began bawling. She began crying hysterically; her chest heaved. I thought she was about to share something no one else knew. It was her moment, but the burden was too much for her. She cried for minutes. The heaving continued as she desperately tried to regain control and composure. She needed to speak. She had to speak. She needed to share. Something was desperately wrong. She needed help.

Although Wendy cried for only about four minutes, to both of us it seemed like eternity. Eventually, regaining as much composure as she could, Wendy just blurted out, "My father is raping me." Again, she broke down and cried hysterically, desperately trying to regain control. For minutes, she tried to stop crying. Her chest heaved and heaved and heaved while her head was buried in her hands. She'd look to the ceiling and squint her eyes as tight as they would go, as if closing her eyes would make her disappear. She couldn't stop crying. It didn't matter anyway. It was out. It was real. It was Wendy's moment.

She regained some composure. The problem was no longer Wendy's alone. The dam had broken. No amount of effort would be able to put that water back inside. She no longer had to hold everything in. The problem was out.

Her boyfriend didn't know. He was just a battered bystander. But that day, someone else was able to carry a part of her load. It was now mine, too. The problem was still there, but her burden was gone.

Wendy slowly opened up. She said she had been molested by her father for years. All four sisters had been molested by her father. As if that wasn't stunning enough, Wendy said she was being molested by him even at twenty-one.

It was obvious that I was out of my league. I could never comprehend her horror or suffering. Her father, her God-appointed protector, had been a predator in her family. My heart was torn for this human being who was suffering an ongoing tragedy. I wanted to hug her, but I knew every touch she had ever had from a male probably felt like the wrong touch. I was stuck watching while my heart ached for Wendy.

How could I bond with anyone who had suffered in ways I struggled to comprehend? I could try to imagine the pain she endured while growing up, but that would be impossible. But Wendy trusted me and chose me as the one to share her story with. I sat and listened. In graphic detail she continued.

I was like a deer caught in headlights. Stunned. I tried to show I cared more than I felt horrified by hearing about her trauma.

Things like this don't happen in our community. These things happen in bad cities and neighborhoods, but not here. It's something that happens to poor families, uneducated families, or stereotypical families from the back hills or third-world countries. But not in my backyard, and certainly not to a nice young woman like Wendy. It was apparent that Wendy's childhood had been lost, and along with it, her self-esteem.

There's no such thing as normal. People may talk of normal people, but they don't exist. Wendy's situation was so far out there, so incomprehensible, that I did the only thing I could—I listened.

As my mind raced, I kept asking myself, *How do I respond? Do I tell my supervisor? Do I tell the police? Do I let her continue to spill her soul out to me? What can I say to someone like this?* Wendy came from a middle-class family in a fairly well-to-do community. I was abhorred at what I had heard. Was it okay for me to tell her I felt disgust, or would she think I was telling her she was disgusting? Would that comment drive her off? Would she feel I was judging her? How could she have let this happen when she was living on her own? Do I tell her my three brothers and I could go over and kick this guy's butt? If she wanted to kill her father in revenge, would that really be too extreme? Did she need help planning a murder?

My head was spinning. I let Wendy continue. She revealed that this had been going on since she had hit adolescence. All of her older sisters had been robbed of their childhoods as well. I pressed her as to why she allowed her father to continue even though she was in an apartment.

Wendy said she had moved out in the hopes of separating herself from her father and the abuse. To ensure she would always be able to afford an apartment, she became one of the best employees at work; failure was not an option.

Wendy said that when she got the apartment, she was excited and, for the first time in her life, felt free from her father's assaults. She kept the blinds shut so no passerby could determine whether she was home. Living with closed blinds would seem like prison to many, but not to Wendy. It was as if she had died and gone to heaven.

The apartment gave Wendy the freedom she wanted. Or so she thought. One day, about a month after she had moved out, there was a knock on the apartment door. She knew that knock. Despite all her precautions, he was back. He had the audacity to try to force himself back into Wendy's world.

The knock paralyzed Wendy. Her heart pounded as if it were leaving her body. She stood in silence and fear. Her father knocked again. "Wendy, I know you're in there." She froze from sheer terror and to ensure no sounds would emanate from her apartment. But he knocked all the more. He was relentless. She dropped to her knees and quietly crawled to her bedroom and then into her closet. "Wendy, I know you're in there."

The knocking continued. Her father had power over her. In the end, he threw down the final words that would ensure his conquest. "Wendy, if you're not going to let me in, I'm going to get it from one of your sisters." It was finished. She was done. Wendy had lost the war. She knew she had been beaten. So slowly she got up, shaking, and walked to the door. She let her father in.

This was probably one of the most devastating times during my short career in clinical psychology. How anyone like Wendy could find a way to believe there was something better in life was beyond me. She said she would detach her mind from her body when her father would rape her.

She envisioned a better life, one without her father. She knew there was something better and clung to that idea even during her father's crimes.

Wendy became one of my favorite clients for reasons I'll delve into later. At the time, however, I wasn't equipped to deal with something of this magnitude. It was too early in my career. I was green. But what made my relationship with Wendy work was that she trusted me. I wasn't there to judge her. Many abuse victims feel guilty, as if they had somehow caused the abuse. My role was to listen to her, to hear her, to understand her, and to help her find a way out. I felt a personal responsibility for Wendy. She needed freedom and gave me part of the burden she had been carrying alone. Her pain was incredible. She needed to escape her prison. She needed a course for freedom and a route for healing.

Sometimes, you just know. At that moment, I knew she trusted me in spite of the fact I was male and was too new to my industry to distinguish my head from my butt. I had a supervisor. But I knew that if I turned her over to another therapist, I would be betraying her. It wasn't ego. I wasn't that good. I just knew she trusted me. I was called for this moment in her life. I could talk to my superior, but I couldn't shift her to another therapist. At that particular moment, that sucked.

This case took an immense personal toll on me. This was supposed to be just a job. I was to use this internship to learn before going off on my own. Counseling 101 tells you not to get emotionally involved with clients. But it was too late. I was in. All in. I didn't have that ability not to be emotionally involved. I wasn't supposed to bring any of this home with me. This would be difficult. I came from a great family. My parents loved me. They challenged me. They had protected me. Wendy's parents didn't protect her. They hunted her. They violated her, tore her down, and abused her. Her father, the one who had brought her into the world, her personal protector assigned by God, had violated her and his other daughters!

To make matters worse, Wendy's mother was in on it. It became apparent that Mom knew of the molestation but had done nothing to stop it. Wendy went into vivid detail about a time her father had his friends over for their weekly poker game. The father had excused himself during the game to go to the bathroom. When her father was gone for more time than usual, Wendy's mother looked for him and found him molesting one daughter in the hallway upstairs. Wendy remembered her mother hitting him and yelling, "Get down to your poker game." Dad got up and rejoined the game. That was it. Mom went back about her business as if nothing had happened. It was clear to Wendy she was on her own. Dad hunted her, and Mom refused to protect her. Neither parent valued her.

By not fighting for her daughters, Wendy's mother was condoning her father's actions. By not fighting for her daughters, she had violated Wendy and her sisters as much as her father had. Mom's actions and lack of protection told Wendy she wasn't worth defending. Each parent had decided their daughters were disposable, of no significance. I will never understand the damage Wendy's parents did to her. It just blows me away.

I don't know how any child or adult could ever be able to let go of something as horrendous as what Wendy had experienced. She had been violated and destroyed by the very people assigned by God to protect, encourage, and nurture her. The only people Wendy learned to trust were her sisters, who were experiencing the same horrible experience. They couldn't protect each other. But Wendy offered herself as the sacrificial lamb to protect her sisters. She would jump on the grenade to protect them. What amazed me was that while neither parent protected Wendy, something internally gave her maternal instincts to protect her older sisters.

Wendy became one of my favorite clients ever. In the end, Wendy got justice. Through quick and decisive action she would assure herself that, the cycle ended abruptly. She took charged. She made a decision to change her life for the better. Admidst desperation and chaos Wendy found the strength to assure her freedom from her predator. Wendy had to deal with issues and guilt and start to find some healing, but her life changed for the better. She gained freedom from the perpetrator and freedom in life, but her healing still probably goes on today. She never had a normal life. Yet somewhere inside, Wendy said to herself, *This can't be all there is to life. There has to be more to life than what I'm experiencing.* She clung to this thought. It drove her forward.

Wendy had no idea of what a normal life was, but she knew her life wasn't normal. Perhaps she had heard girls in her class talk about the good times they had with their fathers. Perhaps they had spoken of their mothers who didn't allow them to do something fun because they wanted to protect them. Maybe she envied other children whose parents would insist on being with them when their friends went off on their own to protect them.

For over twenty-one years, she knew nothing normal, but something inside, deep down, wouldn't let go of the idea that there was something better for her. Her older sisters weren't good examples for her. They never went outside for help. They carried their burdens just as Wendy had until then. The secret stayed in the family until Wendy shared her story with me. She didn't blame her sisters. She knew the gig. Something deep inside kept telling Wendy she wasn't going to be like her sisters. She loved them, but she wouldn't be like them. She could create her own freedom if she could only take the actions necessary to search it out. She didn't know how to end the pain, but she knew doing nothing was a death sentence she wasn't prepared to serve.

In the end, Wendy and her sisters took appropriate actions to ensure their father would never commit these crimes against anyone ever again. At age twenty-one, Wendy had the rest of her life to create the life she wanted. She needed further help to heal and to deal with the tragedy, but she was free to pursue what was in her heart.

Wendy was a protector. Wendy protected her sisters. Through her actions, Wendy protected herself.

Wendy probably grew more than almost any of my patients under my care. I don't attribute that to me. I was no more than a buffer, a light, a sounding board, an encourager. For Wendy to set herself free, she needed to decide four things.

1. Was her life valuable enough for her to aspire to something greater than the torment she lived daily?
2. Did she believe she had a meaningful purpose in life worth living for? Was the potential for her future greater than the pain of her past?
3. Could she let go of the atrocities of the past to have a meaningful future?
4. Was she willing to pay the price to create something great with her newfound freedom? Many people fear that the cost of change is greater than what they already know.

For a lesser woman, the answers to these questions facing Wendy would be no. Her father, her protector, had destroyed the trust parent-child relationships should have. And a reasonable mother would have protected her children no matter what the cost. A reasonable mother would not have sat on the sidelines and assented; she would have taken action. Wendy's mother hadn't. In reality, Wendy should have given up living.

I'm going to ask you to do something dangerous. Think of someone you trust more than anyone else. Think of your favorite person in your life. Think of your father. Think of your mother. It doesn't matter if you're male or female. Close your eyes and imagine that person abusing you physically. It happens to males. It happens to females. Set the book down and visualize the event.

Pretty overwhelming, isn't it? Thank God it's not you. Sure, you can try to visualize what it's like to be that victim, but you won't come close to being within a universe of experiencing what Wendy had experienced. Can you imagine that happening for years and years? Give a sincere thanks to God that the person you trust is so trustworthy and your confidante.

Here's the deal. Bad stuff happens. If someone like Wendy can make a decision that something better awaits her and is worth struggling for, how much easier would making such a decision be for the average person who lives a somewhat normal life?

People waste their lives. They make excuses for why they can't accomplish their dreams. Drugs, sex, alcoholism, shopping, television, video games, and a myriad of other activities just bury the dreams. Television and the Internet occupy their time so the dreams can't resurface. People allow things to occupy their time instead of investing in their passions.

Wendy hungered for something better. She knew something greater was out there. She had heard it from her friends. But as long as she was imprisoned, she wouldn't be able to pursue anything better. She was willing to risk everything for something greater. The decision had been hiding inside for a long time, but it was there. By finally opening her mouth, she took a leap forward.

But you say, "My situation isn't as bad as Wendy's. I don't need to be rescued." But most people need to be rescued from their private prisons. People who are content don't strive for anything better. *Content.* What a nice word that is. So easy to say. It just rolls off the tongue. "I'm content with what I have. I don't need anything more." Those are such weak statements. I'm not talking about being content with what your situation is in life. I'm taking about "content" meaning "not motivated," "lazy," or "uninspired." Weak. Very weak, but we've all been there.

The cost may be too great for some. Giving up comfort or addictions that provide pleasure, even if just momentary, may just be too much for some. Not achieving God's calling for them is a prison in and of itself.

Just because nothing bad has happened to you doesn't mean anything extraordinary has happened either. Any failure to *try* to accomplish what you've been called to do is prison. Failing to step out and pursue the passion deep in your heart is imprisonment.

Your passion can just be a simple as being a great parent or a great spouse (and let's be honest, that's not simple) or creating the next billion-dollar company. It doesn't matter. What matters is whether you believe in something better for you.

Two things separate extraordinary from ordinary people. First, extraordinary people want something more. They know their passions and keep their visions in front of them. They know where they are and know where they want to be and create plans to get there. Ordinary people, on the other hand, don't have a clue as to where they want to be. They live for the basics.

Second, extraordinary people take action. They know their passions are useless unless they take action. They know there is no substitute for greatness. Momentary pleasure and easy, nonchallenging, nonthreatening lives can lead to seeking replacement happiness or ultimately depression.

Some of the best inventions have yet to be invented, but people refuse to move forward with their ideas. They think, *It's just an idea,* or *I don't have the resources to do this,* or *I'm not smart enough,* or *No one will buy what I have to say.* Their excuses are innumerable.

But their ideas remain. They stay locked in their minds ready for the world to hear, but they never happen because they refuse to take action. Good is the enemy of great.

Wendy wanted something better and took action. But you say, "Stopping abuse is not passion." During the abuse and in spite of it, she maintained a high-ranking position in her company while going to college. She was pursuing her passion in spite of the abuse, but to break free from the weight of her tormentor was the final bit of freedom she needed to focus fully on her dreams.

Most people's situations aren't as dire as Wendy's, yet for most, excuses abound as to why they have let their passions gather dust and rot. They should bring out their passions and take action. The dreams they have are still there, waiting to be realized.

Jennifer suffered a similar trauma. She was a world-class athlete. Her story, while much like Wendy's, ends up with lifelong goals being achieved.

Jennifer had been physically abused by her coach for years. He had groomed her and told her parents how awesome she was and that she needed more worldwide competition. Her coach had convinced Jennifer's parents he would look after her while he traveled the world with her so she could compete with elite competition. During all their travels, he sexually abused her. The abuse was eventually exposed, but fell apart when that happened.

Jennifer needed healing. After being freed of the abuse, she was left to carry the horrors in her mind alone. Hotels remind her of the coach. Jennifer would smell something that resembled the certain cologne that her coach always wore, and she'd be paralyzed. The airports they had gone through, the foods they had eaten, the training spots they had visited all brought back crippling memories. In many ways, all her involvement with her sport reminded her of her abuser. The trauma was just too much.

Jennifer wanted to walk away because the better part of her life had revolved around only her abusive coach and training. She had felt so dirty. As a result, the motivation wasn't there.

Friends came to help Jennifer. Real friends. Friends who loved her. Friends who knew what she had been through. The hard part for Jennifer was to believe she didn't have to abandon her real passion of being a champion athlete. For Jennifer, her sport had meant sexual abuse. She had to rewire her brain. The goal was great. Her passion didn't have to be abandoned. The past was the past. The coach was abuse. Her sport would become her freedom, but she had to rewire her brain. Time. Persistence. Faithful friends. Love. All these helped bit by bit.

It wasn't overnight, however. Jennifer cried, hated her sport, and hid from friends and family. She had felt as if the entire world was staring and judging her although she had been the victim. But slowly, bit by bit, she found a new freedom. Her vision became clearer and as a result more personally inspiring. Her new coach demanded a lot of her. He told her that anger, if used properly, could be a good thing. It could help her recapture her dreams that had been ripped from her.

Jennifer recently went on to become one of the best athletes in the world accomplishing goals that no other female athlete in the United States was able to accomplish. She is now the best in the world in her sport.

Jennifer is not healed. It's a process. She'll probably spend the rest of her life healing bit by bit. Jennifer could have spent her next two, five, ten, or twenty years seeking "healing" while missing out on her goals and dreams. Healing and achieving dreams are not mutually exclusive. Although it wasn't easy, she made the decision to pursue her dreams in spite of her circumstances. Doing so became part of her healing process. Jennifer has some healing under her belt. She has championships to boot.

Hopefully, you haven't had experiences as severe as Wendy's or Jennifer's. Even if you have not, things will sidetrack you. Things will challenge you. But the right passion will stir your heart to fight through anything to achieve your dreams. God will place angels in your midst to keep you focused on your passion.

Don't let the past define you. Wendy didn't. She knew a better tomorrow was possible. Your tragic moments will shape you and help you become stronger and more resilient. But your past failures and your past successes aren't your todays or tomorrows. You can, however, learn from them and use them as motivation for something better.

The worst thing that you can take to your grave is potential. Pursue your passion.

LARRY: CHRIST

"Five, four, three, two, one ... chug, chug, chug!" The chants came as I slammed my Mickey's Malt Liquor bottle to the table and raised my hands as victor. It was during my junior year in college. I was on the five-year-and-one-summer program. I had tried every major and found I excelled in socializing. "Socialism" had nothing to do with government or politics; it was the degree I wanted to graduate with magna cum laude.

I had some issues in college. In high school, I wasn't with the geeks, but I wasn't with the jocks. My parents started me a year earlier than my peers so I was a bit behind in stature than my classmates until senior year. Then I grew. When college came around, I worked hard and did well for my first two years. Then I was introduced to beer.

Growing up, I viewed everything as a competition. Being one of four boys, there was always a winner and a loser. On the long, hot summer days after playing sports, we'd come in for Kool-Aid, water, or milk. Each refreshment became a competition. "Who can chug the quickest? Let's race!" I won and I lost, but I learned a skill that set me apart from my peers in college.

In college, my nickname was "One-Beer Bettag" or "One Beer." "Hey, One Beer, what's up?" I'd hear. Over the weekends, people would put money down to see who could chug a beer the quickest. I never lost. Never. I'd win a match, take a few dollars, and be done drinking for the night. One and done.

But one time, I went up against an offensive lineman from our football team. I had never lost. It was just another contest. The money was on the table, and off to the races we went. I chugged my twelve-ounce beer in 1.3 seconds, slammed the bottle down, and raised my hands in victory, fists held high like Rocky Balboa I kicked his butt. Then I saw the lineman raising his hands too. I didn't know how to react. I had never lost, but I had never tied either. This was foreign to me.

Although I was bummed I might have (and I emphasize "might have") tied the guy, I figured everyone would get their money back because of the draw. "Not so fast, Bettag," the leaders said. People were doubling down. I was to have a second beer. A second beer was foreign to me. *You mean we all don't just leave in peace?* I thought. *"This is crazy."*

Everyone was going nuts. I had a stupid fake smile and looked around. *What in the world's going on here? This is so crazy. "Really? A second beer? Can't I just take my money and look for a rematch down the road?*

No, my classmates were kind enough to clue me in on proper beer-chugging protocol. There would be a rematch. Beer chugging etiquette dictates that no one was to leave the room until there was a winner and a loser. *A loser?* That wasn't going to be me. I didn't lose. But then again, I didn't tie either.

The raucous crowd cheered with glee as we were handed green bottles with wide-mouth tops. "Five, four, three, two, one, drink!" they shouted. I drank my twelve ounces as fast as I had my first and looked over to the offensive lineman. Another tie. *Are you friggin' kidding me? A third beer? My word! What's a college guy to do?*

At that point, I started to worry and became enraged. I was mad at myself for tying. I was mad at the rules, which made no sense. But the coed crowd was going nuts, and everyone ran up and down the hall, telling anyone who was still in his or her room to come to the biggest beer war ever. I was pushed and jostled. People were slapping me on the back, saying, "C'mon, One Beer. You can do it." I was nervous. My head was spinning. Not from the beer at that point but from all the commotion. All the money being laid down on the desk blew me away. I smiled some more, but it was the panicked smile you'd have when you'd be about to jump out of of a plan for your first skydive.

By that time, I had no idea who was betting for me and who was betting against me. I saw more money than I'd ever seen before. I'm sure it was no more than $100 on the desk, but all those singles and fives made it look like lotto winnings.

The tight end of the football team got everyone to quiet down. They opened a beer for me and another for my opponent. They were kind enough to make sure we competitors had elbow room. "Everyone back! Give them some room here. Let the games begin" another shouted. "Five, four, three, two, one," and off we went. *You never lose. Finish this guy off and get out of here,* I told myself as I raised the bottle to my lips. My throat opened like a sinkhole and I slammed that beer down in record time. We both chunked our bottles to the table at the same time and raised our hands in triumph simultaneously.

I was truly disappointed. *Another tie,* I thought, but when my friends grabbed my hand and raised it as if I had been Mike Tyson who just knocked out Michael Spinks, I was puzzled and dazed. We had indeed tied, but my adversary had spilled his beer all over his face and down his shirt and chest. Another rule that I hadn't known, but I didn't care. I was crowned the victor.

By that time, the beer had kicked in, and the room was starting to move with me. I knew it was time to leave. With confusing exuberance, I smiled, scooped the money into my fist, and pumped it in the air. I told everyone I had to do something but would be right back.

Back in my room, I locked the door and lay down on my bed. My feet were on the floor, and my cash was in my hand. Within minutes, I was out. Smashed. Down for the count. I didn't wake up until the next day. My feet were still on the floor, surrounded by cash.

A monster was born. A new caricature was created. I went undefeated in college. I'm sure I could hold my own today, but the recovery period would be something else. After my victory that evening, my college life was never the same. From that moment on, I was the life of the party. God was pretty fortunate to have me walking on earth. I knew it. I knew God knew it. But I was irritated that He wouldn't tell me how awesome I was more often. If I didn't go to a party, no real party had been thrown. How could it be since I hadn't attended? Sure, there were get-togethers, but a party wasn't a party until it had received my blessing. I knew it. Others knew it, but God, in my opinion, was a bit slow on picking up on the obvious.

To this day, my friends tell me I wasn't nearly as bad as I have described it (that's why I keep them on the payroll), but my life was a bit of a façade. During my first and second senior year, I was in our college homecoming court. The second senior year, when it was announced I was the first runner-up, I remember being on the field smiling, all the fans in the stands cheering, and others in the court slapping my back. But inside my broken mind, all I could think was, *How come I'm not the homecoming king? What in the world is wrong with me that I'm not the king?*

In truth, the guy who won was a much better put-together person than I was at that point in life and a bit more genuine too. I smiled and congratulated a man much better than me, but my ego and insecurity had run away with me, and I had left behind my core values and my true happiness. Here I was, the most popular guy on campus, but I was miserable inside.

I was dating a girl I'll call Trixie (that's a fun name). She was a great woman. However, while we were dating, my personal deconstruction began. My insecurity was running my life.

One problem I experienced on campus was that there were so many great girls but only one me. I didn't want to be selfish and deny these beauties a great prize like me. It just seemed so wrong to keep myself limited to just one person and deny others. I just wasn't that type of guy. Someone as good looking, dynamic, and as popular as I was shouldn't have prohibited other girls from having the Larry Bettag experience. I made the mistake that traps many men by hooking up with another coed. No, I didn't sleep with her, but making out with someone else meant I wasn't being faithful to someone really awesome.

Trixie heard from a friend who had heard from a friend who had heard from another I'd been messing around. I remember being in Trixie's dorm room when she confronted me and asked me if I had hooked up with Suzie Q. I did the manliest thing I could think of. I denied it.

No sooner had I denied it than a wave of conviction crashed down on me. It was instantaneous, overwhelming, and powerful. I'm sure it was the Holy Spirit breaking me. I admitted to her what I had done. What happened next stunned me even more. I started to cry. Frankly, I started bawling. It was overwhelming. It was embarrassing. It was pathetic.

I know the reason I had broken down. I had been exposed as a fraud to myself. Forget what others thought; I realized I was a fraud. I wasn't being who I always thought I'd become nor who I was supposed to be. I had violated the moral code I had been brought up with.

I grew up with the best parents in the world. They were married at twenty-three and twenty-four and truly loved each other. Not in some made-for-TV kinda way but in a way most people envied. They were a great example. The only thing that I really ever wanted in life was to get married to a wife that I loved and have a wife that loved me. I wanted a lot of kids too. I'd be faithful and would never cheat on anyone, ever! Yet there I was, having just done what I knew I would never do. It was devastating.

I was exposed for who I really was. The pain was brutal. I have no recollection of the rest of our conversation that night. It was a blur. I was a hot mess. I was destroyed. My world had shattered. The façade had been destroyed. Since I saw what I had so desperately tried to hide, I was sure everyone on campus had as well.

About midnight, I snuck into the campus chapel, knelt before the altar, and told God my story. Although God knew the story, I felt I had to tell it to Him. I begged God to repair the relationship between Trixie and me. I remember specifically telling Him, "God, I've screwed everything up in life. I give you my life. Take it over and fix my life and fix me. Just give me Trixie back." It was that night that I truly gave my life to Christ.

It's funny how God works. He gave me Trixie back. She was kind, gracious, and forgiving, but I wouldn't forgive myself. I couldn't forgive myself. I was too far gone. God forgave me. Trixie forgave me. But since I was smarter than both of them, I wouldn't forgive myself. In a very self-destructive way, I became mean to her and withdrew from most everyone.

I would go on walks at night by myself and talk to God, begging him to repair the relationship I had so aptly blown up again. One night, while I was home from college, I went for a two-mile walk. My best friend and I had walked the same two-mile route countless times before. Always under the stars and late at night, he and I would walk and talk about life, love, friends, God, and our futures. There was something cocooning about that route, so that night, I reached out to God.

I spoke to God the entire time and listened for a clear answer. I wanted to talk to God as I could talk to a best friend. I was tired of praying. I wanted him to physically present himself to me at that moment for a sit-down. Just five minutes would be plenty, but I was tired of God hiding Himself from me. God didn't magically appear, and I was furious. Despite my request for a face-to-face sit-down, God didn't play ball with me. He didn't repair my relationship with Trixie (even though He had once and I had blown it up), and He wasn't talking to me on my terms.

With tears in my eyes, I did the most mature thing a new Christian man could do. I raised my right hand to the starry night sky, raised my middle finger, and shouted profanities at God, trying to stir some sort of verbal response from Him.

"You're up there, sitting on your gosh-darn [not the actual words I used] throne, laughing your butt off as you yank my chain for your pleasure like I'm some sort of puppet!"

For the proper affect, I raised both my middle fingers so God could experience a testosterone-laden, double-barrel bird from yours truly.

What a great man I was. In truth, I was alone. I had ruled the world up until recently, but no longer. I was left with nothing but anger. It's ironic that I had abandoned most everyone else and had no one but God to talk to, but I was giving Him one- and two-finger salutes. At that moment, I felt like a pawn God moved around on His chessboard of entertainment. I was ticked off, to say the least, and had had enough of God and his laissez-faire attitude toward me, my life, and my problems.

I repeated the same things to God a few times more during my walk. By yelling and giving God the bird, I was going to hurt Him or force Him to move for me. I was a hot mess. It was a brutal time for me.

I cringe as I write this. I'm not a guy who swears. I don't ever drop F-bombs. I didn't swear in my past, but that night, I had had enough and was determined to show God just how mad I was. God wasn't my enemy. He was on my side. I just didn't know that right then.

I had been raised in a good—actually great—Catholic family. We all had attended parochial schools and never missed Mass. We all loved God, but in truth, I never really knew God. As a kid I had, but there comes a time in our lives when we need to develop our own faith, our own relationships with God instead of being a churchy because our parents made us.

In many ways, God is like a pope or a president or a famous celebrity. Many say they know the president, but few actually do. I knew a lot about God. I knew He was awesome, but in truth, I didn't know Him personally and intimately. That would begin to change after the first night in the chapel, when I gave my life to Christ.

I heard Mike Ditka speak once. He said that for thirty-three years God patiently knocked at his door. He said that God was kind and patient, but he refused to open that door. At thirty three he opened the door to let Christ in and his life began an enormous change.

I had all of these bible bangers in college that I couldn't stand. I loved Christ (even though I didn't know Him), but these guys were junkies and I didn't want their crap shoved down my throat.

When I gave my life to Christ I told God that I would never shove this down anyone's throat. I still hate it to this day. I'll share and people will take what I have to say or they wont, but I'm not selling Christ.

Today, as a more mature Christian I would never dare talk to God like I did the night of that walk. Actually, I hope I'm that transparent always but don't use the language I did then. I'm smarter and more mature, and I know God's on my side. My expletive-laden tirade was just what the doctor had ordered. God knew my heart. God had been waiting for me. As young and dumb as I was in my walk, it was one of the first honest conversations I ever had with God. I didn't reiterate the same words or the same rote prayers. It had been an honest conversation, one from the gut. From the heart. From the depths of my soul. God had been waiting for me. I knew that God was real and had heard me.

Remember that old TV show, *Kung Fu*? David Carradine played the main character who traveled the Wild West while developing his spiritual and martial arts skills. The old monk who was his teacher would say to Carradine, "Ahhh, Grasshoppa," every time he messed up and would follow that with some sage advice.

Just days before that night, I had owned the campus. Days before, I was God's gift to the world. But on that night, I was a broken young man giving God the bird. God looked on me lovingly and said, "Ahhh, Grasshoppa, you are so young and so dumb, but I still love you." I hated hearing that. Hated it. But He was right. We both knew it.

I hated my life but couldn't escape it. I wanted to die, but "thou shall not kill" kept coming into my mind. I knew I wouldn't take my life, but I wanted to be off this earth. I knew that if you killed yourself, you'd go to hell, and I knew the pain I carried on earth was heaven compared to the fires of hell. I was so bummed.

Every night, I would tell God, "I can't take my life, but you can. I beg you that when I go to sleep tonight you let me not wake up and just take me from this world." "Ahhh, Grasshoppa," God would say to me as I fell asleep in frustrated pain. I'd wake up the next morning in a depression, angry at God's indifference to my lot in life.

Pain is horrible. I'm not sure what's worse, physical or mental pain, but when it doesn't leave, it's brutal. You feel as if everyone in the world is moving on and you're not. You're on an island, but everyone else seems so happy. You're lonely and isolated and carrying burdens by yourself. Everyone else is happy but you. You have no one. God has abandoned you. Your friends have abandoned you. You go through the motions, but that's it. Every passing car contains a person happier than you. Every couple sipping coffee at Starbucks is in love and blissful. You see their happiness because, right or wrong, you're so miserable. Depression is a horrible weight to carry. There aren't enough tears to cry.

Often, the worst in life will bring out the best. Most always, you can't see it when you're in it. You're all alone, and the isolation and loneliness are extreme and overpowering. In your eyes, you're hurting but no one else is. It's a miserable place to be in.

After my little event with God, I would party and drink. It took One Beer Bettag only two drinks to forget. But alcohol is a depressant. Within a half hour of drinking my first beer, I would get even more depressed. I quit drinking for about a year since I felt bad enough without alcohol.

I remember one time, my brother, who was friends with Trixie, went out with her to catch up during a college break. Trixie and I were finished, but I begged my brother to help patch things up with us. He said he would. When he went got back, I asked him if he had fixed everything. He said he hadn't. He said she didn't need that. He said she just needed someone to listen to her. I was so devastated. My brother didn't even pitch my case for me.

I got on my bike and rode as fast and hard as I could for miles until I was exhausted. I ended up at a cemetery, spent from exertion. I told God I hated my brother, and I cried. After having no tears left, I told God, "I don't hate him. I'm just jealous of him. He's a better man than I am." Another honest conversation with God, but a bit more mature. God was slowly changing me. "Ahhh, Grasshoppa."

According to clinical psychology studies, over 85 percent of people who attempt suicide but fail are glad they failed one year later. I wasn't going to commit suicide, but I wanted to die. Fortunately, I befriended the best therapist in the universe, God, who patiently gave me perfect therapy.

Over the course of the next year, God helped rewire my brain. My life slowly fell into place, and the effervescent "Lar" eventually resurfaced, but this time with a purpose and grounding. The process was long, but the changes were lasting. God kept saying, "Ahhh, Grasshoppa," to me, but the messages were more positive.

God often uses your painful times to help you grow. Pain sucks, but if you don't deal with it, you can't change. You can bury it through drinking, prescription or nonprescription meds, or antidepressants, but it will remain until you face the pain head-on and move forward. You will come out on top if you deal with it. Consider it God's way of shaping you for something greater. Your pain will mold you and perhaps at some point down the road will impact others.

After college, I obtained a master's in clinical psychology. Because of what I had experienced in college, I was able to connect with clients with severe depression. I could empathize with them and offer them hope. They knew I wasn't a fraud. I had professional training and street cred to boot. I had gone through pain and never wanted to go through it again. But I was glad I had gone through it once. As a result, when others came to me with their great stories of depression, I would get it. Out of the bad comes the good.

I'm not saying that every pain moment will ultimately help others, but I can say that for the most part, moments of pain can mold you into a better person.

Every day during that year, I'd read the Bible. I hadn't been a Bible reader up until then, but I wanted help. Sage advice. Wisdom. When I couldn't sleep at three in the morning, I'd turn on Pat Robertson and the 700 Club.

God was feeding me bit by bit. Just like God did with Mike Ditka, God was slowly reconstructing me.

"Ahhh, Grasshoppa."

In my years of counseling and working in the private sector, I have had a lot of opportunity to talk to people in need. I talk about a relationship with Christ. Not religion, but a one-on-one relationship. Many say they don't know how to talk to Christ. They ask as if there's a magical formula. Sure, God lays out ways to approach Him on the throne, but for someone who has never had a relationship, a real relationship with Christ, it starts with accepting Him into his or her life as Lord and Savior. He is the Great Physician. He healed me. He healed my clients. He heals daily.

But it needs to start with having an honest conversation with Him.

I took a friend of mine to lunch. He had been having an affair, and of course, like most who stray from their marriage vows, he was sad and depressed. He felt he wasn't good enough for God. Although he was right, I reminded him no one was "good enough." It's a myth that you have to be good enough to approach God. You can't and you won't ever be good enough. He said he didn't know how to communicate with God. I shared my story with him. He asked me if it was really true. He didn't believe I had spoken to God that way. "Did you really give God the bird?" he asked. I said yes, but I also said I knew I was growing closer to God even in those moments since I had been honestly seeking Him. I was too young and dumb in my walk for God to care about form. God wanted me, and I wanted help, so we both had to deal with my reality.

I knew God cared about me. I reminded my friend that over the years, God helped strip away the bad and replace it with the good. (He's still stripping the bad away today.) The truth was that I was seeking God. I didn't know Him at that point, but I was beginning to. The process was real, and my seeking was real, and God, despite my imperfections, was thrilled to have me seeking Him. I heard "Ahhh, Grasshoppa" over and over as I got to know Him better.

Looking back, I am okay with the exchanges I had with God. I look fondly on the intimacy that had begun to grow through my conversations with God. Prior to that, everything had been on the surface. Despite my anger, the night of that walk was when I started to fall in love with God. I wouldn't be where I am today without that night.

I stated earlier that the only thing I wanted in life was to get married to a wife who loved me and have a bunch of kids. Without going through that experience of walking and getting angry with God, I'm confident I would have been a multiple-times divorcé. Today, I am married. I love my wife (most of the time). She loves me (sometimes). I have five kids I love (I'm a masochist), and they seem to love me a lot (they're not that smart). I'm living the life I had always hoped to live, but without God's demand on me to mature a bit, I wouldn't be in that position today.

If you want to do great things you need an awesome partner, preferably someone smarter than you. By partnering with God you become Ben with Jerry or Jobs and Wozniak, or even Sears with Roebuck. One couldn't do it with the other. When I die, you won't be there to defend my case. When you die, I won't be there to plead your case. It's all about you and God. Create that partnership today.

It's said that Thomas Edison, a great inventor, lost all his inventions in a barn fire. Thomas called his kids to see the magnificent fire. One said, "But Dad, all your inventions are in the barn!" Thomas retorted something to the effect of, "Most of those inventions were crap. I have some good ones I can redo and make better, and I have great ones in my head, but a fire as great as this you'll never see again."

In my leadership role at work I didn't like conflict. If major problems contained conflict, they would linger for weeks or even months. Rich

Brennan, the president of The Brennan Method, used to do personal and professional coaching with me. He shared the Thomas Edison story with me and said the point was that we should "run toward the fire." This changed me forever. I still don't like conflict, but I have become a person of immediate action. I won't carry burdens for months by refusing to address the source of conflict. By running toward the fire, by running toward the problem, I assure myself I won't be carrying the burden for long because the resolution to a problem is imminent when that problem is faced head-on. Problems I used to carry for months now disappear in days. It's refreshing and creates a deep inner peace.

This was a process. Ahhh, Grasshoppa. Day by day, week by week, year by year, God slowly built me back up. I regained much of my innocence and with that, joy. It took me years to learn to run toward the fire. God continues to work on me today.

"Ahhh, Grasshoppa," he continues to say to me.

Things will happen in your life. Like me, you'll probably be the creator of many of those problems. Problems you didn't create will still be forced upon you. You can deal with them by running toward the fire, or you can avoid them and carry them for as long as you choose.

God will equip you so you can overcome your deficiencies and emphasize your strengths. But none of that can happen without knowing Him. And you have to know him intimately. You will never be good enough to approach God, so get those thoughts out of your head. It begins with an honest and true conversation with Him.

Ahhh, Grasshoppa.

DAVID: MOVING FORWARD

One of my favorite historical figures is David of the Old Testament. He resonates in my heart in so many ways. I identify with him because of his courage. By no means can I compare myself to him with greatness, but I can compare myself to him in respect to distractions, shortcomings, sinfulness, selfishness, and God's forgiveness and second chances. I probably mastered shortcomings better than David did.

After he slew Goliath, David became King David, God's favorite. God called David a man after his own heart. In Acts 13:22, NEW INTERNATIONAL VERSION God said that he "made David their king. God testified concerning him: 'I have found David son of Jesse, a man after my own heart; he will do everything I want him to do.'"

After his victories, David was praised by the people and was drowning in riches. There he was, just a little shepherd boy who overnight became the Elvis Presley, Michael Jackson and Justin Bieber of his time. David got a bit lost with his power.

One day, after having settled into his role as king, David was on the roof of his penthouse suite and saw some serious eye candy bathing a few rooftops over. Although he didn't have binoculars, he saw enough to think, *Daddy likey, Daddy wanty.* So David phoned a friend who knew someone who knew someone who knew the woman, Bathsheba. He invited her over to see a movie and to show her his fish tank, and the next thing you know, Bathsheba was pregnant.

Scandalous? You bet. Only he and Bathsheba knew what had gone down. Maybe a few of David's innermost peeps, but really, no one else knew. If anyone else knew, no one told him, "Dude, bad idea. You can have your pick of the litter from all the single kittens, but this chick's already married to a cool dude in your army." Nope, his posse just let David do his thing.

The stuff was about to hit the fan in a real big way. David was not sure how to hide the story. Bathsheba's husband, Uriah, had been off at war. So a pregnancy wasn't possible with Bathsheba's husband. Bathsheba had an impeccable reputation, as did Uriah. David knew that and feared a couple of people might have seen her being escorted to or from his palace. He knew that something needed to be done before TMZ broke the story and it appeared on the front page of the *Jerusalem Times*.

In his sleepless nights, he came up with a plan. He invited Uriah to his digs. The following conversation ensues:

DAVID. Thank you so much for coming at such short notice.

URIAH. Anything for you, my eminence.

DAVID. Uriah, I hear you've been rocking it on the frontlines of our army.

URIAH. Thank you, my king. I'm at your service.

DAVID. Forgive me for being so rude. Beer? Shot? Tequila? No? How 'bout a glass of vino? I got the best stuff around.

URIAH. Thank you, my king, but I'm still on duty. I can't right now.

DAVID. Okay then. Well, let me get to the point. Word on the street is you're tearing it up in our army. Word is you're kicking it. I can't tell you how proud I am of you. Seriously, you've got some big stones, dude.

URIAH. Ummm, okay ... uh ... thank you, my king. I'm trying.

DAVID. You're to be rewarded for your faithful service to me and our nation. Why don't you and the missus spend some downtime hangin' with each other? Consider it a gift of gratitude from me, Israel, and the people of our country for all you've done for us. I can get you a great place at the Jerusalem Astoria. All expenses paid. On me. Gratis. You can have the honeymoon suite to boot. Kick it with the missus, if you know what I mean. Just my little way of saying thanks. Here's a jar of my best wine. Go and celebrate with Bathsheba (wink, wink) dude. You've earned a bit of R&R.

URIAH. Wow! What can I say? Thank you, king, but I'm on duty, and my focus is on serving you at this time. I can't really take time off until my time is up.

DAVID. You don't get it, bro, do you? I need my best men functioning fully. With what I'm hearing from you, I need you at your best. You've been burning it at both ends. Great men like you and I need to take a bit of time off every now and then, wouldn't you say? It keeps us sharp when we are on the job, no? I need my best men sharp always. A little bit of downtime will do you good.

URIAH. Thank you, king, but I took an oath to you to serve you. I'm still enlisted. I can't have downtime, at least not during my call of duty. Don't get me wrong, but I made a commitment to you and to all Israel that I'd do my duty. Also, as a side note, I'm really clicking on all four cylinders right now. I'm in the zone. Forgive me for being so bold, but I don't want to ... er ... blow the mojo I have going on right now, you know?

DAVID. That's why I love you, Uriah. You're so dedicated. But here's the gig. I'm king. You're not. If I want to take care of my top people, that comes with my title. You're one of them. Head home, drink, celebrate with your wife, and come back rested and sharper than ever. That's an order.

URIAH. Ahhh, er, yes, king. Whatever you say.

Uriah went home and celebrated with Bathsheba with a nice dinner, but really, he wasn't thinking of hooking with his honey. He knew he needed to be sharp. He couldn't let the king down. There would be time for celebrating after his call of duty was up, but it wasn't that day. Downing some vintage vino and hitting it at home really sounded good, but Uriah knew it would take him off his A game. He'd lose his edge despite what King David said. Despite the king's orders, Uriah went home, but he was faithful to the oath he had sworn when he enlisted.

David got word and in frustration tried repeatedly to set the mood for Bathsheba and Uriah, but all to no avail. One time, David had a feast with Uriah and got him drunk and sent him back to sleep with Bathsheba. But again, Uriah crashed with the servants of David, refusing to get with his wife.

At that point, David realized if Bathsheba went outside to tan in her Israeli bikini, people would start asking about the baby bump.

Desperate times called for desperate measures. David moved to plan B. Check this out. David understood his role as God's servant and emissary. So David thought, *I gotta whack him. I need to have him offed.*

David couldn't locate Don Corleone, so he told his five-star general, Joab, "Next time you're at war, put Uriah on the front lines. Then, in the heat of the battle, pull back on him. I need you to leave him alone and isolated."

Of course, Joab was going to obey because he didn't want to be next on David's short list. He also surmised that Uriah must have done something really bad. After all, David was the protector of the people who didn't put hits on people without good reason. No argument from Joab. "Yes, King David," he responded as he slowly backed out of the throne room. Joab put the king's plan in motion.

Long story short. The fighting ensued. Uriah was put at the front of the line, and sure enough, the army pulled back. Uriah was killed.

David got word that Uriah has been killed in battle, fighting for his king. David did the most noble thing a murderer could do. He sent flowers to Uriah's funeral and had Bathsheba move in with him. Purely out of compassion, of course.

In 2 Samuel 12, God sent his prophet, Nathan, to visit David and tell him a story to seek David's wise counsel. Nathan skipped all introductions and began telling his story. He said there were two men in a particular town. One was rich, and the other was poor. The poor man had just one sheep he loved dearly. With all his life. The rich man, however, had an entire flock of premium sheep. The best in the country. The rich man came upon the poor man and wanted the poor man's one sheep. The rich man took the sheep.

David was incensed. He burned with fury at the man who had no compassion for the poor man. Nathan basically blurted out, "That's you, David. You have a harem of the finest honeys in the land and you go and take Uriah's wife. You took his love and you killed him on top of that."

David, feeling shame, confessed his sin and admitted to wrongdoing. Nathan told him God forgave him, but among other consequences was the fact that David would lose the child Bathsheba was pregnant with.

The child was born and immediately became sick. As his son lay dying, David prostrated himself before God and begged for his son's life. He could hear his servants whispering among themselves. They were afraid to tell David the bad news. They said, "He didn't listen to us before, so how can we tell him that the child is dead? He may do something desperate" (2 Samuel 12:18). NEW INTERNATIONAL VERSION After finding that his son has died, David got up from the ground. After he had washed, put on lotions and changed his clothes, he went into the house of the LORD and worshiped. Then he went to his own house, and at his request they served him food, and he ate.

His attendants asked him, "Why are you acting this way? While the child was alive, you fasted and wept, but now that the child is dead, you get up and eat!"

He answered, "While the child was still alive, I fasted and wept. I thought, 'Who knows? The LORD may be gracious to me and let the child live.' But now that he is dead, why should I go on fasting? Can I bring him back again? I will go to him, but he will not return to me." (2 Samuel 12:20–22)

Really? David dressed in his fine duds and went to the temple to worship God, who had taken his son's life. He knew the gig, and here's what is most important. The past was the past. It couldn't be undone. For David, it was time to get on with God's mission for his life. Brutal past. Horrible crime. Horrible sin. He asked for forgiveness, but it was time to move on.

Here's the thing. Here's what's most critical. In the Bible, God said, "David is a man after my own heart." Really. God wasn't speaking about David's sinfulness, although I'm sure God was fully aware of it when God called him a man after His own heart (Acts 13:22). David had the heart of a lion. The heart of a warrior. David sinned, just like you and me. We all sin. Sure, David's sins were over the top and scandalous, but a sin is a sin is a sin. David paid dearly for his sin. God wasn't pleased with David's actions. He made David pay dearly for rebelling against Him. But at the end of the day, despite David's sin, he was a man after God's own heart.

This was one of the most liberating messages God has ever taught me. Here's why. People beat themselves up all the time. They beat themselves up for their shortcomings. I've always beaten myself up for my sins, my mistakes, and my every failure. I'll ask God for forgiveness, and I know He forgives me, but I don't forgive myself. I bring out my noose and hang myself over and over. I won't forgive myself universally. I'll forgive myself on some sins, but not on all of them. Not on the big stuff. If David didn't move on beyond these major sins, the Bible wouldn't read as it does today.

But every time I bring out the noose to hang myself after God has forgiven me, I'm dealing with my next sin. Arrogance. It keeps me from moving forward. If God forgives me, I need to forgive myself and move on, but often I don't. I carry it with me, and it's a burden carrying my sin. It's as though God's forgiveness wasn't enough and I feel I can find some sort of justification for carrying my last sin.

The failure to forgive myself hampers me in three ways. First, I'm refusing to accept what God has already done for me. He's washed my sins, but I live under the burden of the sin by not forgiving myself.

Second, I can't move forward since I'm carrying a burden I wasn't meant to carry. If God forgives me but I won't forgive myself, I must be smarter than God. Since I know that's not the case, I have to deal with my arrogance. It took me long into my adult life to be able to forgive myself and to look forward instead of beating myself up for my sins.

Third, by refusing to accept God's forgiveness, I'm making myself smarter than God (been there, done that plenty of times). *Sure, God has forgiven me*, I say to myself, *but God has no clue as to how badly I sinned. If He only knew how badly I felt about my sin.* As a result, by refusing forgiveness, I'm deciding God doesn't know about my sin, or if He does, He doesn't realize how badly I sinned.

Ultimately, David was restored.

> Then David comforted his wife Bathsheba, and he went
> to her and made love to her. She gave birth to a son, and
> they named him Solomon. The LORD loved him. (2 Samuel
> 2:13–24)NEW INTERNATIONAL VERSION

If I recall, Solomon turned out to be the wisest man ever. A prodigy. A gift from God. If David refused to move on, Solomon may never have been born.

Bottom line? David sinned. Did some bad stuff. He realized this and repented. He paid a price for his sin, but he humbled himself with sincere sorrow. God forgave David. David didn't look back. God restored him.

Satan is known as the great accuser. He wants you to feel bad. The Bible says God removes our sins (when we repent) as far as the east is from the west (Psalm 103:11–13). On a horizontal line laid across the earth, there is no end to the east and there is no end to the west. God continued, "I will remember their sins no more" (Hebrews 8:12, 10:17). NEW INTERNATIONAL VERSION

God accepts our repentance. We are reprimanded and taught by God, and God moves on by remembering our sins no more. Here's the problem. God doesn't erase our minds. And that could be a good thing if used right. The Devil, the great accuser, loves to remind us of our past failings and of what a loser we are. David had the stones, even after losing his son, to get up, praise God, and move on.

The Devil doesn't want us to forgive ourselves. It's the Devil's tool. Why would he need to interfere in our lives when we can hang ourselves? Here's the thing. David pleaded for his son's life. All to no avail, but after David's son died, he didn't mourn. Upon his son's death, he moved on. He took his punishment like a man and moved on with God's mission for his life. What had been done had been done.

Past sins are good to remember for the purposes of learning and growing, but not to hang yourself on. When I get in similar temptations in life, I remember my past sins. They remind me I shouldn't sin again. We are all imperfect. We will sin every day of our lives. If we were without sin, we'd either be God or we'd be dead. We must ask for forgiveness, confess our sins with sincere repentance, and move on to the plans God has called us for.

Don't get me wrong. This isn't a carte blanche to sin and say, "Such is life." You need to make headway against your sin and leave each one behind. Use the memory of them as motivation to not sin again. Deepen your relationship with God. Become better and stronger in your walk with God, and turn from your sins and your vices. As long as you're doing that, you will move forward without looking back. The Devil wants you to hang yourself daily and be so consumed with your shortfalls that you never move forward and accomplish what God has called you to accomplish.

It's impossible to move forward when you're hanging yourself on your past. Many try to bury their pasts by masking the pain with drugs, sex, alcohol, video games, or shopping or whatever. Anything used to bury the past will keep you off your path. Derailed.

There is a huge difference, however, between letting go of the past and burying the past

avid let go of his past. All his actions were done. He fell prostrate before God, asking for his son's life to be spared. He begged for forgiveness. Like many of us, he bartered with God and promised Him he'd be a better man if He spared his son's life. Here's the deal. He faced and dealt with his past. He dealt with his sins. He addressed everything head-on.

Those who bury their pasts end up carrying them. How heavy is that? Can you imagine carrying five-pound rocks in each hand for the rest of your life? You can do it for a while, but after some time, you would be looking for relief. That's what a lot of people do. They look for relief if even for a moment. All they have to do is let go, but they choose to carry their rocks.

Letting go of the past means dropping those rocks. David did. The rocks he carried were twenty pounds apiece. He dealt with them head-on. He knew God had a mission for him. He also knew he couldn't carry those rocks forever. It was just too difficult. That's what made David a great leader. He wasn't perfect. On the sin scale, the judges had given him perfect tens. What made David great was that he knew in order to move forward, he would have to let go of the past. A very conscious decision on his part.

He knew word had gotten out. Those who used to cheer him would jeer him, call him a fraud, a fake. He would ride his chariot in the crowds and see the women gossiping. The men knew that while they weren't kings, they were better than David. David felt certain the stares of adulation had turned into looks of distrust and doubt, but he pressed on. His mission was clear. He dealt with it with God, and he would certainly deal with it in life and in community.

A friend of mine pled guilty to a felony. It was a financial crime. He is married and has three children. As of this date, he hasn't been sentenced, but he's looking at three to five in a federal penitentiary. When everything came to light, he ran. He wouldn't deal with his sin. He hid. He wouldn't go out. He knew people were talking. He was sure everyone who looked his direction was judging him. For sure they were talking about him.

I told him that it didn't matter, that God had a great plan for him. He would argue, "I feel like such a loser. Everyone is looking at me and telling me I'm a dirtbag." I told him it didn't matter what people said. Those who abandoned him weren't his friends in the first place. They never were. The conversations went on for months. Eventually, he decided I was right. He's not the first. He won't be the last. I told him, "Those who are obsessed with you are missing their own calling."

Our sins might be worse than David's. Maybe the fact we waste our talent and time is worse. David didn't waste his talents. He sinned big time, but he got back on track to fulfill his mission quicker than most people who are content with carrying five-pound rocks.

Others have risen from their scandals. Michael Vick of the Philadelphia Eagles spent time in prison for running a dogfighting ring. He asked for forgiveness and sought counseling and became a star quarterback in the National Football League. Other sports stars such as Brett Favre, Deion Sanders, and Ray Lewis dealt with scandals of integrity. They knew the stares would come, but they didn't care. They wanted to get back to their missions.

Others escape by looking for momentary pleasures for solace. The television becomes their best friend. But by finding solace in moments, they sacrifice fulfillment. They sacrifice dreams. Dealing with issues in public is too great a fight. That's sad. There's not one person who hasn't dropped the ball. We all have. It's just whether we will drop our rocks. That leads to victory. Holding onto them leads to emptiness, desperation, and despair. There can't be enough moments to replace abandoned dreams and goals.

Let's give the Devil his due. When friends forgive us, and God forgives us, Satan still sits around pointing his fingers at us, reminding us we failed. God remembers our sins no more once we confess them, but the sneaky little snake comes in during bad moments and reminds us we're just a bunch of losers. The worst. We fell today, and when we were down, he gang tackled us and threw every past failing and sin onto the pile.

There comes a time when you need to tell the Devil to "pound sand" and focus on God and the path He has set before you. I use stronger words when I recognize what's going on. I'm not shy when it comes to telling the Devil to back off.

When you fail, just confess, move on, and ask for more strength. You have a lot to accomplish on your mission. Get better. Look forward. The past is relevant, but only to learn from, to grow from. Don't wallow in past mistakes, past imperfections, and self-pity. Self-pity is pathetic. I've drowned in it. I'm sure you have too, but let's be honest; who do you know who wants to hang out with someone who has his or her head hanging on the ground 24/7, weighted down with self-pity? Gross.

The past doesn't deal solely with sin. There's anger. I could write a book on anger. I should write a chapter on anger, but suffice it to say I'll only make mention of anger and its effect on you.

People who have been wronged carry anger like their skin. They just can't get away from it. They stay mad at family members, parents, kids, friends, and coworkers who have "done them wrong." Fortunately, for whatever reason, anger hasn't been one of my issues. God has given me plenty of other issues to deal with, so I'm grateful I don't carry anger around.

Here's the deal with anger. Often, when we remain angry at others, it's to hurt or to punish them. Our feelings were hurt because of others' actions. Two things happen when we carry anger around. First, those we're mad at often have no clue we're mad at them unless we let them know. That doesn't stop us from carrying the anger. If you have the need to harass the other person because of your anger, you have issues bigger than what my little commentary can deal with. I'll save this topic for my next book.

The second and more important reason to eradicate anger from your life is that anger will sabotage your dreams and goals. If you're so focused on how you've been wronged, how can you focus on your heart's dreams? Impossible. It derails you from bigger things. Don't let anger do that to you.

Finally, when it comes to anger, it's not like you haven't wronged someone else. We all have. But you say, "Yeah, but I did only *this*. This person did *that.*" A sin is a sin is a sin. Forget it. Move on. Let God have your anger and get moving on with your plan. You can obsess over how you've been wronged, or you can obsess about pursuing your calling.

In any event, your past can't be undone. God can restore your marriage. He can restore your financial or physical health, but sometimes that doesn't happen. Sometimes, He will provide the opportunity for restoration, but you can't get in a place to make it happen. It doesn't matter. Today matters. Your future matters. Yesterday matters only to learn from. Yesterday's failures and successes mean nothing today and tomorrow. Learn from the past. How you decide to act from this day forward will determine how quickly you'll succeed in God's plans for you and if you're able to move on to the next, greater mission or conquest.

Once you regain your innocence, the garbage that interferes with your plans for life will be flushed away. You can get on to what you have desired for your life. Doors will open. Your mind will become receptive to thoughts and ideas about how you can utilize your skills and gifts to achieve your greater purpose. You will regain your passion for life. Life is so much better when you're looking forward, not backward.

FEAR OF CHANGE

I saw many women like Jane during my short career in clinical psychology. Jane came to me because she was being physically and mentally abused by her husband. The physical beatings weren't often, but they were consistent enough that she could predict when the next one would arrive. Every few weeks or so. Just when things seemed to be going well in her marriage, something would happen, an argument would ensue, or he would be drinking, and *bam*, he was all over her. When she'd drop and break that plate or not prepare the right meal, when she messed up, she knew a beating was coming.

The cycle was pretty simple. She'd screw up. He'd beat her. In terror, she'd lock herself in her room, but he would kick the door open and hit her. Initially, she fought back, but eventually, as the fists kept coming, she quit fighting and put her head down to protect herself. He would leave, and she would lie on the floor crying. She would rarely go to the emergency room because that would prompt the questions she didn't want to answer. She wouldn't go out in public for a couple of weeks after a beating unless she was wearing long-sleeved shirts and dark sunglasses ... just in case.

In her time of isolation, she knew this was so wrong. But still she loved him. This wasn't the man she had married. He had once been so kind and charming. *It must be me*, she'd rationalize. Sometimes, she threatened to leave, and the husband would "come to his senses" and settle down. He'd promise her he'd change. He would win her back. Wine and dine her. "Let's go to a movie. Just you and me," he'd say. He'd beg for forgiveness.

Jane recalled he had been under a lot of stress. After all, she remembered, he had been such a good guy. She knew she shouldn't have done that one thing that irritated him. Having little to no self-confidence, she would believe his accusations that she was the cause of her beatings. Was it her lack of self-confidence or the fact that she wanted to really believe that, this time, he would change?

Invariably, she told him she appreciated his efforts and would think about it. *Got her*, he'd think. He'd have relief that his bride was back with him. Although her tension left after his promises, the adrenaline was also leaving, and she was soon realizing she wasn't happy, and worst of all, she was all alone.

One time, while she was feeding her youngest, he came home from what must have been a horrible day at work. Just looking at him told her not to approach him. *There's that look*, she thought to herself. *Make things quiet and get him a good meal. He'll feel better.* She cringed as her child kept crying. She prepared the best meal she could for him, but she smelled the alcohol on his breath as she gently set the plate before him. She was beginning to get scared. He knew it too. He could see her fear. The shark smelled blood. How he hated her at that moment.

Jane said, "Let me know if you want anything else. I'm going to get Bobby ready for bed." She scampered out of the kitchen, praying she wouldn't hear from him.

Eventually, the clicks of knife and fork ended. She heard his footsteps. They weren't the usual steps. The pounding feet elicited fear. Those steps told her it was time to take cover. In the nick of time, Bobby was put down in his crib and covered with a blanket. It gave her just enough time to sneak out of his room and quietly shut the door. "You must have had a bad day, honey. Do you want to watch football or something on TV?" she asked.

Wham. He shoved her against the wall. *What did I do now?* she'd ask herself, and the cycle started again.

When I met with women who suffered from such domestic abuse, I realized they were paralyzed by fear. The fear of the unknown. There was more security and peace in the fact they knew the cycles; they knew that after the beating there would be peace. There would be calm. Their husbands would try to love them. But if they left, then what? The unknown. The fear of the unknown for most of these women was so much greater than what they knew. There was comfort in the cycle. The unknown caused paralysis.

The few women I counseled who left abusive situations and forged forward on their own felt confidence they hadn't felt in years. Initially, it was rough for them. The separation, loneliness, and lack of self-esteem was brutal. Sure, they were moving ahead, but their initial steps were painful. Psychologically, the initial separation was pure torment. Their initial time of freedom and security was spent battling low self-esteem and codependency.

Eventually, each woman who left an abusive situation came to realize she had power. This inner sense of strength had been gone for a long time, but it resurrected itself albeit slowly. The little seed inside began to bloom again, which was thrilling for them. All women are wonderful in God's eyes. They were made with a purpose. Some of those women came to understand that. They came to feel joy and freedom in growing in the way God had intended.

Many times, the guy would reach his own personal desperation when a woman who had never left before was leaving for good. He'd beg and promise to change. Some women went back, but many didn't. I'm not advocating divorce, but let's be honest here. No woman made in the image of God needs to take physical abuse.

How about your fear? You believe in your heart you've been called to do something great or extraordinary, but it's so new and foreign that you too may be paralyzed with fear. Completely. How are you going to do it? How are you going to start the process? What if it fails? Yet the dream remains. There comes a time, as it does with abused women, that a decision has to be made. It's never too late. Do you pursue your dreams and make the world a better place in spite of fear of the unknown, or do you bury it, hoping something great will happen in your life without your decision, your action? Don't be buried in a casket along with your potential. Never take your potential to your grave.

One of my best friends used to joke, "Do something, even if it's wrong. Just do something." We'd say that when one of us was starting to annoy the other and wanted the other to go away. But we would have serious talks about how many in our office were just hoping that business would walk in without effort. Coworkers hoped business would miraculously show up. Thus his remark, "Do something, even if it's wrong."

Many people are waiting for lottery tickets instead of using the winning lottery numbers God created in their DNA. He's given all of us the goods. We all have the winning numbers, but we need to put it to use. It will require a lot of effort. Nothing easy becomes great. Nothing great becomes easy. So the choices are polar opposites. Ease or greatness? It will take a lot of effort, but the reward for those of us who are faithful is over the top. They'll find freedom, and their self-confidence will boom.

They'll take their beatings along the way. Challenges, obstacles, and nay-sayers, but standing on that mountaintop, well, there's nothing more gratifying. Abraham Lincoln had to fight for everything in his quest to change the nation. He was defeated almost every time he ran for office. He spent more than a year in bed fighting depression, but he got up. He fought on and suffered more defeats before becoming one of the best presidents of our country.

It's not when and where and why you're knocked down but how you respond. When you fail, go ahead—cry, feel sorry for yourself, have the world's greatest pity party. But the next day, get up. Move on.

Fear battles opportunity. Change battles opportunity. Good battles great.

My high school teacher, Frank Bucaro, held a class on death and dying in which he spoke about studies on people who died and were brought back to life through CPR or other methods. Some said that when they died, God replayed their lives. Their entire lives. Every second for them to see from birth till death. God said, "This is how I intended for you to live your life," and He played their entire lives as He had intended them to live.

In all cases, the people stated they wished they had lived the lives God had chosen for them. I don't know what happens after death, but if there were only one chance in a billion the same thing would happen to me, I'd want to live my life to the fullest. That means I deal with my fears forge on. I relentlessly chase my calling with purpose. I have taken plenty of beatings. But I love where I am today in relation to where I was.

Unfortunately, our society looks for the easy way out. That means safety. That means little conflict. It also means very little fulfillment. Low growth means low fulfillment. You don't have to be an inventor, an author, or a world-class speaker, but it does mean you have to shake the dust from your dream that today is only potential.

Some might read this as a "name it and claim it" book. That's not true. This is probably more along the lines of "use it or lose it." In Matthew 5:14–29, Jesus gave a great parable about a man who, prior to leaving on a trip, called three of his servants and entrusted bags of gold or talents to each. To the first he gave five bags of gold. To the second he gave two bags, and to the third he gave one bag. When he returned, he called each to account for the gold he had been given. The recorded conversation goes something like this:

SERVANT 1. Boss! You're back! How was your trip? I have so much exciting news to tell you. I invested your money. You'd be stunned at what I was able to do.

BOSS. Wow, you're really exciting me. Tell me more!

SERVANT 1. Boss, I invested some of the money in the local market, some in farming, some in camels—but I won't bore you with the details. Let's just say the five bags of gold you gave me … well … here they are back and, ta-da … here's five more. So whaddya think? Pretty hot, huh? You won't believe the contacts I made when you were gone. I know you have a lot of catching up to do, but when you have the time, let's sit down. The opportunities are driving me nuts.

BOSS. You da man! That's why I gave you so much in the beginning. I knew I could trust you. Great job putting the money to use. You're going to share a lot more with me in the future. C'mon bud, I want you to celebrate my happiness with me, and after our little soiree, I want to hear all you have to say. This is exciting. Thanks for tackling this head-on.

Servant 1 leaves high as a kite. His mind is racing. He's thrilled he did so well and just as happy his boss is happy. He can't wait for the next meeting. Servant 2 walks in.

SERVANT 2. Um, hi there, boss. Hope you had a great trip. Just wanted to say I missed you. A lot. Um, ah, can I say this was an interesting time for me? You know, I've always felt I could take on a challenge like this, but I haven't been in a situation like this before. I wanted to talk to you for some advice, but since no one will even know what a telephone is for another 1,900 years, I just had to go it alone.

BOSS. Wow, sounds like you had an interesting experience. Well? Go on! But before you do, I missed you too! It's great to see you, but don't keep me in suspense. Spill the goods.

SERVANT 2. Um, well, like I said, this was so new to me. Really foreign in many ways. I was nervous but excited. I thought, *What if I lose the money?* But then I decided it's better to have tried and lost than to have not tried at all. I figured even if I lost everything, you'd be gracious enough, or at least I kept telling myself that. My only rule was don't be foolish with the money, but alas, I keep digressing here.

BOSS. No, No, it's all good. This is fun. You know something, you hit a key that most people don't get. You tried. Of course I don't want to lose money. And you're right, don't do something foolish, but I gave you what I gave you because I believed in you. I trusted you. You know that, right?

SERVANT 2. Yeah ... yeah, of course I knew that (cough, cough).

BOSS. Well, I did. Do you think I'd recklessly throw my money away? No way. I need people who I believe in to take and work with it. I can't do it all on my own, and that's why I gave you the two bags. Go on.

SERVANT 2. Ah, thanks, boss. Um, here's the short version. You gave me two bags, right? Here they are back, and, ta-da, here are two more. You won't believe what I did to earn this, but let's just say you're now involved in The Dead Sea Harbor Port. You're into manufacturing shields for the army. And we're opening a fast-food coffee chain in downtown Jerusalem. Can you imagine waking up, walking to the market, and having someone else make you a cup of java? Seriously? Sounds weird, but it's a big hit in the market. Not too shabby, if I say so myself. Here, I bought you a mug of the stuff. In any event, you go on a trip and come back for a 100 percent return on investment. Sorry ... I can't contain myself. Can I say just one last thing?

BOSS. Hmmm. When they invent cars, we'll have to consider a drive through, but yes, of course, this is exciting for me too. It blows me away. But yes, do tell.

SERVANT 2. Well, I'm really glad I made that money. It was really cool to see it go to work. Awesome, actually. But the two biggest kicks I got out of this was how much fun I had doing it. It's not so much the money, it was the learning and growing and the challenges along the way that were the coolest. I had so many moments of frustration. Some were brutal. But I learned so much. I have a confidence I always wanted. I guess I just want to say thanks for this experience. I mean it.

BOSS. Wow! Well said. Can I say you've been good? You've been faithful to your task. I thank you too. You amaze me. I will trust you with more, but for now, come party and celebrate my happiness with me.

The second servant exits. Everyone in the room notices his feet don't touch the floor. He floats away, thrilled at having the experience. The boss says, "It's been a good day. I need to call Servant 3. He'll be the icing on the cake." Servant 3 shows and sheepishly smiles.

SERVANT 3. Hey, boss! Good to see you! How was your trip?

BOSS. Awesome, really a great trip. And I've been filled with nothing but great news since I came back. Am I excited to talk to you! I'm thinking you're going to make my day with your news. I can't tell you how excited I am to see you. So tell me, how'd it go?

SERVANT 3. Thanks so much for the kind words. I think you'll be pleased. Check this out. Times are tough. The market and economy in Israel aren't what they used to be. We're always at war with our neighbors, and things seem so unsettled. So, I got to thinking ... Can I be frank here, boss?

BOSS. Yes, please.

SERVANT 3. When your name comes up on the street, everyone says you're the top dog. You reap where you did not sow, and quite frankly, you're just one tough son of a gun. So I thought to myself, *Why don't I be the bank? I need to protect my boss's money. I'll keep it from the people who have it out for you.* Check this part out. I buried the money. People couldn't steal it because it was underground. I put my donkey's bed on it so no one would get at it. I protected your bag of gold. Not exciting by any means, but it's protected, 100 percent. It's all here. Sorry about the dirt on the bag, but that stuff's gonna happen protecting your money the way I did. Whaddya think?

Boss. Wow. What can I say? Is it okay if I'm frank with you too?

Servant 3 (*smiling smugly at boss*). You bet! Bring it!

Boss. Thanks. I don't know how to say it nicely, so let me be blunt. You did a terrible job, horrible.

Servant 3 (*blood draining from his face*). But ...

Boss. I gave you your time to speak. Now I get mine. You're as lazy as they get. By your own words you hang yourself. You knew that I—what was it?—"reaped where I did not sow." So shouldn't you have at least put the money in a real bank so I could at least get interest off it? Really? That's as good as you got? I don't believe it for a second. Sell it to me all you want, but you don't have buyer with me. You're lazy and you're wicked. You've wasted the talent you'd been given. Guards, take the gold from him and give it to Servant 1 and take this one away. Get him out of my sight. I'm done!'

The talents can be money or simply the gifts God has given you. If you're not using them, you're wasting them. The only fear in your life should be the fear of being lazy and not utilizing God's gifts and talents. No laziness. No complacency. Remember, there are no rewinds in life. What's done is done. Move on. But no matter what, don't waste what's been entrusted to you.

Fear will come. As in Jane's case, there is so much fear of the unknown. But the alternative is regret. I'd rather have fear than regret. I can work my way through fear. I'll get tense, but there will be a bit of adrenaline released at prime moments. Regret, though, can be released, but it can't be undone. What you've missed out on, you've missed out on. No thanks. I'll live with fear instead of regret. So will you.

FAITH: GROWING OR DYING

Sunday, February 16, 2007, was a beautiful winter day at my home in Saint Charles, Illinois. My brother-in-law, Scott, had come over to our house with two snowmobiles. Our property was just under two acres, not conducive for an all-day snowmobile run, but it would be just the perfect entertainment for my three children—eight, six, and four—and some cousins for an hour or two. Michelle had them bundled up in snowmobile coats, knit hats, and mittens. Scott had one snowmobile, and I had the other.

One by one the attrition began. One cousin went in because he was cold and wanted hot chocolate. One of my kids went in. Another got tired. Someone else got bored. Brett and a few of his cousins continued on until the short day began to dim.

I had announced last run to Brett, who was lying on a plastic sled behind the snowmobile, I'd told him he'd get a double run and then we'd call it quits. Brett lay on the sled and awaited his run.

The snowmobiles were about twenty-five years old. They were in great shape, but they didn't have the zip they had had in their heyday in the early 1980s. Also, two acres was a large lot for a house, but no great speed would ever be achieved on them. To top it off, all the trees on our lot were more reason to go slow.

I opened the throttle and off we went. I zoomed around the yard and did a U-turn for his final turn. As I came around the last corner of the house, I zigged when I should have zagged, or zagged when I should have zigged. Either way, Brett went off the track and into a clump of birch trees. I turned around and saw the sled was gone and I was pulling only rope. I hoped the rope hadn't whipped him in the face. A piece of the sled was still attached to the rope. *Cheap plastic sled*, I thought. *We weren't even going fast.*

I circled back. Brett was face down in the snow, not moving. He was crying through snow-caked eyes, tears seeping through the snow. I picked him up, set him on my lap, removed his glasses, and wiped the snow from his face.

There's an unwritten rule that when a kid gets hurt, you give him or her two minutes to regain composure and shake it off. But Brett wasn't cooperating with Parenting 101. He continued to cry. I felt bad for Brett since he wasn't one to cry. The others did, but not Brett. I knew something was wrong.

I told him to stand up. He wouldn't. He just kept crying. I again told him to stand up. *Shake it off*, I thought. Obediently, Brett slowly rose but buckled back over in the snow in pain. I asked Brett where it hurt, and he said his stomach. My grandfather, father, and three brothers are all medical doctors. I worked at a nationally renowned outpatient surgery center for three years and knew immediately that Brett had major issues. Something happened to Brett internally. Brett was not a hypochondriac, a malingerer. I later told my wife that if it had been his younger brother, Jake, who had taken that tumble, he would have died. For the first six years of his life, Jake cried about everything. This was Brett. This wasn't normal.

Brett should have had a surface injury like a bruise or bleeding or something, not pain in his stomach. My limited medical experience told me that the pain meant internal bleeding. To what extent, I didn't know, but I had to act quickly.

I carried him to our home. I brought him inside and took off his snow pants. Michelle asked me what was wrong. I said, "I'm taking Brett to the hospital. He's hurt."

I wasn't going to wait forty-five minutes for paramedics to come and analyze him and strap him down just to take him to the hospital to begin the process all over. It was probably pretty stupid, as he could have been paralyzed or something, but I wasn't that smart at that moment. All I could think of was taking action. I told my wife to call the ER to let them know we were on our way.

I remember being in the car. I felt Satan was trying to crush me with guilt. I told God that I was sorry, that I had been careful, and that I wasn't going fast. I told Him what was done was done and to please forgive me for whatever recklessness I was responsible for. I told God I would needed forgiveness immediately so that I could focus forward to help Brett I couldn't focus forward by hanging myself for failing Brett.

When we got to the ER, I gave them the lowdown. They let him pass the other people waiting in line. I knew this was serious. The medical staff obtained blood samples from Brett and did chest X-rays and CAT scans and all those other tests they do in the ER. The doctors said he had torn his spleen and was losing blood fast. The doctor ordered a blood transfusion while I was standing there. They said he would probably need a splenectomy, a surgery to remove his spleen.

I was stunned, but for some reason, I knew this was a spiritual challenge. I had spent years studying faith after I had asked Christ into my life. I believe some are called to "specialize" in preaching or teaching or love, but God had me focus on faith. I excused myself, went to the bathroom, and locked the door. On the bathroom floor, I prayed alone. I told God I wanted

His best for my son. I told God that He had appointed me as custodian of my eldest son, a child He had given me, and that I hadn't protected him. I knew that the firstborn son held a special place historically and that Brett was my firstborn son. It's not that God wouldn't do the same for others, but I told him Jesus was his firstborn son and I was my parents' firstborn son and Brett was my firstborn son. If the injury had happened to Jake or Claire, I'd come up with something else, but since I was an attorney, I had to lay out my arugment and case before God in prayer.

I told God that since I had failed to protect Brett in my role as a parent, it was up to Him to fix him. I reminded him of John 10:10: New Internatianal Version "The thief cometh not, but for to steal, and to kill, and to destroy: I am come that they might have life, and that they might have it more abundantly." I knew Satan's purpose was to kill my son and destroy our family and my marriage. My sister's daughter had survived leukemia. As my sister was counseled during her three years of dealing with her daughter's leukemia, she discovered that the vast majority of couples who go through such ordeals end up divorced because of the trauma and shock to the family. Translation: Satan will use anything to destroy a family, even the sickness of a child. But I also knew God is all about abundance, miracles, healing, and hope.

I read a book by a great preacher, Ken Hagin. He illustrated our problem with working with God that I found useful during my time of prayer. Could you imagine a person who has a million dollars in his checking account but tells the world how poor he is, that he never has money for housing, transportation, even the basics? All he had to do was write a check to meet his needs. The Bible, Ken Hagin says, is the same. God's deposited in your account all His promises in the Bible. You just need to write a check on those funds. The Bible is the Word of God, but too many Christians don't know the promises in the Word or how to draw on them. Even worse, many Christians know God's promises but fail to act on them.

I felt doubt because of the words of others. People would say that he was in God's hands and that if God wanted Brett to keep his spleen, He would, but it was up to God. Friends and medical staff would say, "No matter what the result is, God will take care of Brett." I can't tell you how many times I heard this during this event. To me, it was, *No flippin way! The ambiguity of God's will is whether I should take this job or marry this girl or buy that house.* Ambiguity, prayer, direction, wisdom, and counsel are for the things God doesn't address in His Word. The things God says in His Word I'm taking as true. Maybe I'm crazy, but I need something somewhere I can hang my hat on. If it's written clearly in the Bible, there should be no "if it's the will of God" in prayer. Doubting when things are clear contradicts what's written in God's Word.

With regards to healing, I believe God is fully behind it. To me, having an eight-year-old needing blood from someone else or having his spleen removed was not God's best. It's second best at best. It's acceptable, but not God's best. Too many people don't draw on what's in their account. I needed to. To me, Brett wasn't going to lose his spleen sitting in the pediatric intensive care unit just because I didn't fully protect him. So while on my knees in the bathroom behind closed doors, I told God I had been sold out to Him for the longest time in my career as His follower. I reminded Him that like Samuel's parents, I had committed Brett to Christ at birth and at that instant was recommitting again to Him right there in the ER. I told God either His Word was true or it wasn't; either I was going to tell others about the strength and power of God's Word or I wasn't. It wasn't a threat; it was just that my entire walk with Christ had emanated from the fact that God's Word was truth. God said, "Put me in remembrance of my words," in Isaiah, so I did as I reminded Him of His words and truths.

A blood transfusion and a surgery to remove a spleen were acceptable, but it wasn't God's best. I wanted only God's best for my son. For crying out loud, God had given me Brett to take care of. I wanted to be the best advocate for my children.

However, in all humility, I told God I wouldn't jeopardize my son because of my ego. Faith has many levels, and God says you can tell a mountain to get up and move if you have faith the size of a mustard seed, a very tiny seed. My faith in God's Word was so much greater that day than it was the night I gave my life to Christ. No, it wasn't an ego issue. It was a fact issue. But as an attorney, I felt I needed to present my case to the judge, or in this case, the Great Physician. But if, in fact, it was medically necessary, I would acquiesce to the doctors and allow the transfusion. I always said okay whenever a doctor told me it was likely Brett needed his spleen removed.

A medical staff member walked in with a Styrofoam container of blood for Brett's transfusion. The ER doc came into his room and said, "Okay, we have the blood, but we'll hold off for now. We're sending the blood in the helicopter with your son, and if his blood counts drop further, we'll give him the transfusion en route." I said okay to that and quietly, secretly, again reminded God I wasn't going to move from what I believed in spite of what I saw and felt. My mind and feelings were racing with doubt, but I told God what I expected and told Him I'd stand on what I had prayed to God. My challenge was walking by faith, not by sight.

The helicopter flew Brett to the pediatric hospital, where new doctors repeated all the processes. I stood my ground and reminded God I did have faith the size of a mustard seed (Matthew 17:20). I told Him to help the little faith I had. Again, the doctors relented. They said they'd continue to watch his blood counts before doing a transfusion. I didn't want a transfusion. I have an attorney friend who contracted hepatitis with a transfusion. Transfusions are acceptable, but I didn't want anything latent in the blood. I wanted God to just work within Brett's own biological makeup.

Eventually, Brett was stabilized, removed from the ER, and sent to the pediatric intensive care unit, the PICU, Mark 9:28-29 came to me came to me.

After Jesus had gone indoors, his disciples asked him privately, "Why couldn't we drive it out [referring to an evil spirit that the disciples tried to cast out, but only Jesus was able to cast out]?" He replied, "This kind can come out only by fasting and prayer." New International Version

I felt the Holy Spirit telling me I had to fast to ensure Brett's recovery. I don't know why it came to me, but I wasn't about to argue with God. This passage wouldn't leave my mind. That verse kept coming to me. I finally relented and told God I wouldn't eat until Brett got to eat. "I'm putting myself with Brett," I told God.

The next day, Brett ate some Jello, and so even though I knew Brett wasn't healed, I used Brett's sucking on Jello as an excuse to go to the hospital cafeteria, where I chowed as if I hadn't eaten in weeks. I knew inside I had rebelled. I felt God's leading but used Brett's Jello to rationalize my eating. Within a couple of hours of my disobedience, all of Brett's vital signs had greatly deteriorated, and they wanted to perform an emergency procedure to drain fluid collecting under his lungs that was forcing him to increase his heart rate to extreme levels and lower its capacity to pump oxygen.

I guess I hadn't had the right heart about this fasting thing. I repented and told God this time I really wouldn't eat until Brett got to eat solid foods. Later that night, I went outside his room as he slept and opened the Bible to Psalm 66: NEW INTERNATIONAL VERSION"Honor the vows you have committed to [reminding me to stay with my fast]" and later in the same Psalm, "God has surely listened to and heard my voice in prayer." It was at that moment, days later, that I knew victory was mine despite what I saw or felt from that point on. God gave the healing to Brett. I just had to wait and watch for it to manifest in Brett's body.

Doubt came and went after that. I hadn't seen any great manifestation of healing, but I didn't care. Brett was still in the PICU, and his vitals went to extremes from time to time over the days of his stay. Every time his vitals dipped, the nurses bypassed the pediatrician and called the surgeon. Every single dip in Brett's vitals would lead to an action that would that would tick me off or challenge me spiritually further.

During this time, God reminded me of Daniel 10:12–13. NEW INTERNATIONAL VERSION

> Do not be afraid, Daniel. Since the first day that you set your mind to gain understanding and to humble yourself before your God, your words were heard, and I have come in response to them. But the prince of the Persian kingdom resisted me twenty-one days. Then Michael, one of the chief princes, came to help me, because I was detained there with the king of Persia.

God had heard my prayer. I just had to stand and resist doubt. It seemed that the angel on my left shoulder and the devil on my right were playing ping-pong and my brain was the table. No, God had heard my prayer. Doubt came and went in this extreme battle. This verse reminded me to pray without ceasing and to continue with my fast.

I had two extreme moments of doubt in my head that thankfully never made it to my heart. I was able to nip each in the bud. By the time Brett was discharged, his vitals had gone through many more extreme ranges, each time resulting in another emergency page to the surgeon. As time went on, I became less moved by what I saw and more solid on what I knew to be facts. God's words.

My son has his spleen. He's home. He won't die of some disease due to not having a spleen to filter bad bacteria. Brett will be a better man than me someday. He has my testimony, and so do you. My faith has grown by leaps and bounds. I'm sharing this with my fellow believers so their faith may be strengthened as well. I was challenged but overcame and am stronger because of it.

I hope this serves to strengthen you in your walk with Christ and in your desire to open and share the secrets of God's power. No matter what your issues are in life, God has probably spoken about His will in His words.

You will go through times when no one but God can help you. The doctors did the best they could. I had zero power to undo what had been done. All I could do was to feed on the strength God had given me. I relied on what I knew. I walked by faith, not by sight. When those moments come, you will rely on the strength God has placed in your heart. His words. His signs. You'll carry forward even though others say what you want is impossible. Trust me. There will be times when no one else knows, no one else understands but God and you. When you come out of those moments, you'll be glad that you stand as victor.

MICHAEL: PASSION

They were just Converse high tops, but to the gangly sixteen-year-old, they were the world. Think of today's Air Jordans. His parents didn't have a lot of money, so those Converses were an extravagance.

He pulled on each row of laces from the toe to the top making sure they were tight. *Make 'em snug*, he thought. *Tie 'em tight*, he told himself. The tryouts in ten minutes would be his time to show he belonged in the starting rotation. He was determined to be a starter. He knew all the summer pick-up games, the late nights shooting with little light would be worth it. That day was payday. He always played with the older guys and held his own. His older brother saw it too. He could hang with him. But he'd have to show coach what he already knew.

After tightening his shoes, he grabbed his basketball, stood up, and took a deep breath. He filled his chest with as much air as it would take and slowly exhaled. Pounding the ball against the locker room floor, he walked to the gym. Inside, he looked around and dropped his ball. Walking toward coach, he heard the whistle blow. It was time. Time for his tryout.

The tryout went well. He missed a number of shots, but against other sophomores, juniors, and seniors, he more than held his own. He did better than most. *Not bad*, he thought. He knew he could have done better, but he knew he had done well enough to impress his teammates and the coach. Although he was only a sophomore, he knew he belonged. *Finally, he thought, all this hard work has paid off.*

For a week following the tryouts, he anxiously waited for coach to put up the starting five and hear his name as the starting guard. He'd waited a long time for this opportunity. His best friend told him the roster was up. Both ran to the school as fast as they could.

On the inside of the gym door window was the list of the coach's final decision. Waiting anxiously for the juniors and seniors to leave, he finally pushed his way to the front. Scrolling up and down the list, he searched for his name. No Michael?

There must have been some mistake. His name wasn't there. It wasn't on the starting five. In fact, it wasn't on the sheet at all. He hadn't made the cut for the varsity team. While his friend saw his own name on the list, Michael Jordan couldn't find his name. Sure, he was only a sophomore, but he belonged. He knew it. There had to be some mistake.

Though his friend was elated, he didn't want to celebrate too much. MJ wasn't on the list. He wouldn't even be riding the pine for the varsity. Nada.

Tears welled in his eyes, but he'd play it cool in front of his friends. He knew he could do that; he had game. He felt he had had a good showing on the court. *None of those guys are better than me. Okay, maybe I shouldn't start, but I definitely should be on the varsity team.* Maybe his teammates were better than he was, but he'd have none of it inside. Michael forced a smile and told his friend how happy he was for him. He began his long walk home. By himself.

The tears were behind a dam that had to break. After the first one came, the rest burst out like a water balloon stuck by a pin. He sobbed and heaved. He didn't want anyone to see him cry, but he couldn't contain himself. He ran as fast as he could to take shelter inside his house. Michael knew he belonged on the team, but instead he was looking for solace, alone.

Sneaking into the house, he went to his bedroom and locked the door. He crawled into bed and let it all out, drenching the pillow with salty tears. He was devastated. He could scream and cry in his pillow and no one would hear.

In many ways, this became a defining moment for Michael. The world's greatest basketball player cut from his varsity team. Sure, he was a sophomore, but he knew he had the goods.

Would he wallow in self-pity? Would he think this wasn't the sport for him, or would he rebound? The devastation was real, but the next choice was his, not his coach's or his parents or his friends or his teammates. A hundred percent all his decision. *Not good enough? Really? Maybe coach knows something I don't. Maybe coach didn't know anything.* The tornado in his mind spun faster and faster.

As he sat there with his face jammed in his pillow, the angel on his right shoulder and the devil on his left argued.

DEVIL. You don't belong in basketball, Michael. You were cut from the team. Cut, Michael. If you were good enough, you'd at least be riding the bench, but you were cut. You say you're so great. Big stuff? The only thing big here, Michael, is your ego. Coach is right. You don't belong on the team. Move on. You can't even make the bench, dude. You suck.

ANGEL. Michael, bad things happen to great people. This is your defining moment. Every great person has these moments. Only losers allow the moment to define them. What will you do? Rise up? If you work harder than anyone else, no one will ever cut you from any team ever. You want this, Michael, and you know it.

DEVIL. Ha, ha, ha—what a bunch of malarkey. You hear what this angel's saying to you? How bad do you want it? I know people who want to make a lot of money, but they don't. I know people who want to save their marriages, but they don't. I know fat people who want to be in the Olympics, but they aren't. You're a sophomore in high school, MJ, so go and hang out with your friends. You worked this hard for what? For nothing. What a waste. Forget all this hard work. Hard times and hard work for you are over. It's not like you'll ever do a TV commercial or anything.

ANGEL. It all comes down to this one word, *passion*. Everyone has passion. Some keep it. Some fuel it. Most bury it. But passion alone won't take you where you want to go. You see, God gives each of us gifts. So many people squander them. Wasting your gifts would be the greatest tragedy, Michael. You're a hard worker, but this next year, you'll work harder than anyone else. Don't quit. Remember, success is driven by failure. For those who utilize failure correctly, success will abound. You have that passion, and it will drive your work ethic. Use this failure and your passion to motivate you to work harder than everyone.

DEVIL. Let's be honest, Michael. Those are really nice words, but that's all they are, words. You were cut from the team. Cut! You may not like coach at this moment, but you and I agree coach doesn't cut people for the sake of cutting them. Coach isn't begging you to knock on his door. No one else is saying you're *all that*. Only you are. I have news for you, Michael. Someone has to give it to you straight. You're good, just not that good. If coach saw any talent in you, you'd at least be watching on the bench, But really, if there's no talent, move on!

And so the argument went. Good versus evil. Blow by blow, it was a champion MMA match taking place in Michael Jordan's head. *Will I? Won't I? Should I?* Finally, in unison, the angel and the devil shouted in stereo, "What's your decision, Michael? We need a decision!"

Eyes swollen and bloodshot, Michael slowly peeled his face from the matted pillow and rolled over on his bed. He lay there for a few moments, staring at the ceiling. He didn't want to get up. He was spent. But ever so slowly he wiped his eyes and exhaled. He sat up only to throw himself down again and stare at the ceiling. He repeated this once more before shifting over and throwing his feet over the side of the bed.

His head hung low, he stared at the floor while he wiped his tears. He didn't have many feelings left, but raising his head ever so slightly, he saw it in the corner. It was looking back at him. The devil and the angel didn't know if he had seen a friend or an enemy when he saw that basketball, but both sat there, ringside, to see what he'd choose. That bald basketball smiled and smiled. *Dude, we got some work to do, don't we?* the basketball seemed to say. Michael didn't smile back. He wanted to kick that basketball through the side of the house. *Are you a friend or foe?* he thought as the basketball kept grinning.

He picked up the basketball, spun it in his hands backward, and bounced it. He stood up and headed outside. The passion was still there. No other person was going to tell him how good he was or how good he was going to be. The decision had been made, and it was his. That devil hung his head and left the Jordan house to prep for another day, another victim.

Without passion, it's almost impossible to succeed. Without passion, you can have moments of success, but great accomplishments take great passion. Talent and passion are completely separate. There are so many people who have talent but no passion. Passion will take you to your ultimate success. Motivation gets you going, but passion gets you there. With passion, your eyes never leave your goal.

I have practiced clinical psychology, law, and mortgage banking. My employers at Cherry Creek Mortgage are wonderful and inspiring leaders. They have invested a lot into my personal growth. My bosses are mentors and coaches. I have hired a number of professional coaches over the years.

Coaching has become critical to my success. No one succeeds alone. Great people have outside counsel. Michael Jordan had a coach. Tiger Woods has a coach. LeBron James has one. Bryce Harper, Aaron Rodgers, Roger Federer, Rafael Nadal. They all do. All great ones do.

Coaches help keep their "coachees" on task, honing their skills and keeping their eyes on the prize. They help perfect and prune. They help fuel and channel passion.

I have come to realize my passion is helping people. I love helping others look inside. I like to watch the awakening they have when they discover there's something better for them. That enthralls me.

Writing this book has been another passion of mine. I have wanted to write it for years but had the same devil and angel sitting on my shoulders, one telling me, "Go for it," and the other saying, "You suck. No one wants to hear what you have to write."

But the best part is when you realize, as did Michael, that passion will take you from your defeats to your victory. Motivation never will. Motivation dies. Passion persists. Passion is from the heart.

I worked at a basketball camp with Michael Jordan, I was in college and MJ did two basketball camps every summer. One was at his hometown in North Carolina, and the other was at my college just west of Chicago.

My brush with fame was working that week with Michael. I was the head lifeguard and, after the basketball camp ended each day, the attendees were allowed to swim for an hour before heading home with their parents. One day I was walking in the athletic center with Michael and we had the following exchange:

Me: Michael, why don't you come swimming?

Michael: No way, I don't swim.

Me: Come on Michael, I'm a swim teacher. I'll give you free lessons.

Michael: Uh, Uh, I don't want to drown

Then I pumped both hands in a victory position above my head and shouted "I can do something that Michael can't." Michael, with his head lowered, just shook it back and forth and smiled as I ran into the athletic center with glee.

probably the best basketball player ever. However, his successes hadn't made him so great, his failures had. What he did with his failures defined his path and history.

For a weaker person, being cut would have meant questioning a passion. Not Michael. Michael was cut from the team, but he never wavered in his passion and determination to become a great player.

After winning the first of six NBA championships with the Chicago Bulls, Michael decided at the end of each season how to improve his game and become better. He was already the best basketball player on the planet. No one could cover him. No one was nearly as good as him. Still, he identified parts of his game he needed to improve. He wanted to get better.

After being the scoring champ in the league and becoming the league's most valuable player, Mike determined he needed to become a great defender. He became the defensive player of the year in the NBA in 1988. Already the best, Michael wanted to get better.

Michael turned fifty not too long ago. His personal trainer, Tim Glover, said that even today, at age fifty, Michael could score fifteen to twenty a game. With his passion and drive, I believe he'd still have stellar moments.

Just think what the world would have missed out on had he not picked himself up after getting cut from the team. Failure happened, but it didn't define him. It motivated him, and his passion kept him focused. He would never be cut from the team again.

Michael's stats:

- 6 times NBA champion (1991–1993, 1996–1998)
- 6 times NBA Finals MVP (1991–1993, 1996–1998)
- 5 times NBA Most Valuable Player (1988, 1991–1992, 1996, 1998)
- 14 times NBA All-Star (1985–1993, 1996–1998, 2002–2003)
- 3 times NBA All-Star Game MVP (1988, 1996, 1998)
- NBA Defensive Player of the Year (1988)
- NBA Rookie of the Year (1985)
- 10 times NBA scoring champion (1987–1993, 1996–1998)
- 3 times NBA steals champion (1988, 1990, 1993)
- 10 times All-NBA First Team (1987–1993, 1996–1998)
- All-NBA Second Team (1985)
- 9 times NBA All-Defensive First Team (1988–1993, 1996–1998)
- NBA All-Rookie First Team (1985)
- 2 times NBA Slam Dunk Contest Champion (1987–1988)
- NBA's 50th Anniversary All-Time Team
- #23 retired by Chicago Bulls and Miami Heat

If Michael had lost his drive or had listened to the naysayers, the haters, the doubters, the sports world would have been less exciting. Nike wouldn't be as prosperous. We would be without Air Jordans. There wouldn't be any "I wanna be like Mike" Gatorade commercials.

You believe there's something greater for you. You have a passion that's over the top. But nothing will take you there except for your drive. No one else may understand your passion. It doesn't matter. It's your passion anyway. If your passion is clear, you'll remain true to your calling. You need to know your passion. Define it. Own it. Everyone's passion is unique.

Those who want to conform are expected to give up their passions because they don't comport with what's perceived as normal. And normal you are not. That's the way God has designed you. Instead of conforming, you embrace your passion with a singleness of purpose. It's your passion, and it should be your drive.

Learning from Failure

We learn but little in this life from success.

Success leads the ego, failure chastens it.

Success makes you look up, and the sun dazzles you;

Failure forces you to look down and mind your own step.

The man who can fail and learn, who can
try and fall and get up and go on,

Who can make a new start and be defeated and still go on,

is the man who succeeds in the end.

—Harold Hayden

ERIC: PERSISTENCE

March 13, 2007, was a day that changed the lives of my parents and siblings forever. Michelle was six months pregnant with our last daughter, Tessa. We had just finished a school function that night. The weather was beautiful, and I thought it'd be a great time to stop by the Oberweis ice cream shop on the way home to end a nice spring night.

Michelle and the kids all ordered ice cream. I indulged in my favorite, a chocolate malt, easy chocolate with whipped cream and a fancy swirly cookie. As we sat outside, we relished the beautiful weather that early in the season. I thought this was living. Considering the size of our family, fancy ice cream shops were an all-too-rare treat.

About halfway through my malt, I received a call. I don't remember who called. Either my mom or my sister. I learned my brother Eric had been in an accident. I wasn't too worried because we've all been involved in minor accidents, fender benders, from time to time, so my concern was nominal.

"How is he?" They didn't know. An ambulance was on the way. "Ambulance?" This wasn't good. I told my wife Eric had been in an accident that sounded fairly serious. We needed to go.

I raced Michelle and the kids home. In the interim, I got word that the accident was bad and that he was being airlifted to Loyola Hospital in Maywood, Illinois just west of Chicago. I helped Michelle for about five minutes with the kids and zipped off for the one-hour drive to the hospital.

Eric is the fourth of the five Bettag sons and daughters. I have always called him "Rock." He was a tough son of a gun growing up. An all-star lineman in high school. As my younger brother, he was my counterpart in family rebellion. My two other brothers and sisters were perfect. Two became doctors, and my sister graduated number one out of Notre Dame's MBA program. Me? Not so much. Eric? Not so much. We were our parents' projects.

Eric provided a lot of levity to the family. He loved to push my parents as far as he could. A family of seven needs a spectrum for great synergy. Most of us had a lot of fun growing up in our family, but Eric and I took it up a few notches. In fact, Eric passed boundaries even I thought no kid should pass.

My grades were average at best growing up. Eric was almost held back in fifth grade not because of intellect but because of BS He'd BS the teachers about this assignment or that assignment and then come home and BS my parents about the teachers. Fortunately, both saw through Eric, and he was able to not have to repeat in grade school but not without a bit of drama.

Later, my parents were told by "professionals" that Eric had a learning disability. Our parents would have none of it. For them, it became a problem for which they had to find a solution. Eric wasn't going to be a great doctor or a businessman, some teachers would say. He'd just have to work harder, which really meant that Mom and Dad would have to ride him like a mutha. Eric, with my parents holding a cattle prod, ended up fighting through all these issues, graduating college, and earning a doctorate in podiatry. A doctor, a podiatrist.

While in podiatry school, Eric married his college sweetheart, Joan, and started having children during his medical training. He worked his butt off, graduated, opened and built a practice, and grew his family to five children.

But here it was in March 2013, at the end of another long day at his practice. Eric had seen his final patients and was on his way to the annual party at the surgery center on whose staff he was. He pulled out of his office and headed to the party. He was enjoying a cigar when the light turned green. He accelerated through the intersection. He was hit. Blindsided. By all estimates, Eric's big Ford Excursion rolled at least five times before running up against a telephone pole.

Once the rolling stopped, he smelled cigar smoke, but it wasn't in his hands. He didn't know where it was. He didn't know what had happened. Regaining his senses, he tried to climb out. But the strangest thing happened. He couldn't move. He saw the sunroof and wanted to climb through it, but his body wasn't listening to his brain. Within seconds, Dr. Aguilar, a gynecologist whose office was next to Eric's and who was heading to the same event, came running up. He called my father, an anesthesiologist, and the host of the party that evening. "Jerry, Eric's been in an accident. It's not good. Get down here."

Fire trucks and paramedics arrived in minutes. They couldn't remove Eric because of the car damage, so they brought out the jaws of life, a super saw that cuts through anything, including a Ford Excursion. Eric remembers having something put on his face to shield him from sparks as they cut him out. Dr. Shoener, a general surgeon, showed up. He hopped in the ambulance and rode with Eric to an open field at a local forest preserve where a helicopter was waiting for him. Dr. Shoener told Eric to move his toes, his legs, but he couldn't. Eric heard Dr. Shoener tell my dad this was really bad.

They loaded him for the half-hour flight to Loyola Hospital in Maywood. For the first time since the accident, he felt relaxed. It was finally quiet except for the hum of the helicopter's rotors. Just a quiet hum, giving him moments of quiet and peace.

At Loyola's ER, he started getting angry. The doctors and nurses kept asking him the same questions. "What's your name? What's your birthdate? What's your wife's name? Tell me your Social Security number." The questions were repetitive, relentless. He was tired and upset, but the questions kept coming.

He was taken for a CT scan. His wife, Joan, and my parents showed up. Mom called a priest to give him last rites. Eric said he knew he wasn't going to die, but still, his family had arrived, and he didn't care if a priest came or not. Everything was a blur.

During my trip to the hospital, I didn't know Eric's condition. I prayed God would spare his life. I told God the reasons:

1. He's a great brother with an over-the-top sense of humor.
2. He's a great husband.
3. He's a great father.
4. His patients loved him.
5. His five kids aren't even in high school, and they needed him.
6. It would devastate me and would all but destroy our parents.

I argued on and on. Though I was repetitive, I was sincere. His life had been spared, but there was a question about paralysis. He had fractured his spine and didn't have feeling or movement in his lower extremities. Although he had full range of movement in his arms, he lacked fine motor skills and dexterity in his fingers.

After the CT scan, he was taken for surgery to stabilize the front of his neck. And that was it. He was out. The general anesthesia let him finally sleep. The next day, Eric woke up. He was incensed. He was angry. No one was there. He was by himself with all these doctors and nurses. He wanted the staff to leave him alone. He wanted his family. To make matters worse, Eric had a neck brace on, so he couldn't move his head. He stared at the ceiling. The nurses turned on the TV. March Madness was going on, but all he saw was the ceiling tiles and an occasional smile from a nurse. The anger burned. They told him to eat. He'd have none of it. He wasn't hungry. All he wanted was to be left alone and to rest. Everything else was meaningless.

When Joan arrived, Eric yelled at her for not having been there. She said she had left because the doctors said he had received enough anesthetics to sleep for twelve hours. He had slept for only eight. He was so mad at her, the doctors, and his situation. *Why me? What did I do to deserve this?* The demons had arrived. Their torment began.

My other brothers, medical doctors, showed up with Dad. They read the CT scans to try to make sense of a bad situation. The doctors said Eric would never walk again. A guy who had just run a marathon would never walk again. He'd never use his hands. One doctor saidsaid that he'd be a vegetable. After a second surgery to stabilize the back of his neck, the neck brace would be removed.

After three days in intensive care, Eric was moved onto the main floor. The nurses gave him a hand buzzer if he needed anything. *How absurd*, he thought. *I can't move my hands, so why bother with a stupid buzzer?* Hospital protocol? Perhaps, but very demeaning. It just added fuel to his anger. Joan stayed to help with his needs. He was moved to a room with a drug addict who cried incessantly and didn't want Joan in the room. The hospital's visiting hours ended at night, and Joan had to go. She would leave, but when no one was looking, she'd sneak back into his room and sleep on a chair. The nurses turned a blind eye when they saw her curled in the uncomfortable chair sleeping next to her husband. Love was fighting back.

The next day, a dear family friend, Father Tim Seigel, drove to Chicago to spend time with Eric and give him last rites. Since moms always know best and Eric was in no position to argue, Eric allowed the priest to administer the last rites and to pray with Eric.

I was there when they had to move him from his bed to a gurney. My dad, the nurses, and I handled that. He said it was the worst pain he had ever experienced. People were pressing on the surgical incision. It was brutal. Rock began to cry. My heart was breaking seeing this. I wanted to cry, but I couldn't allow myself to in front of Eric. Eric didn't need to see that from anyone. But the pain. It was unbearable.

One day, he and I were alone. I talked with him about hope and God. He got the whole God thing but was so frustrated. As a doctor, he could speak MD and knew what the gig was. He said, "I'm not going to live like this. I know how to make it look like an accident. I'll give it one year, and if I don't like where I'm at, I'm out of here. No one will know, but I'm gone."

I was glad he gave himself a year. This wouldn't be Eric's legacy. He was a fighter, but for me to see this was tragic. It was something so new to Eric and me. It was overwhelming for both of us. But time proved this was just a moment, not a destination.

His situation was brutal. I never expected his attitude to be a bed of roses, but I didn't expect him to be that down either. His depression was as deep and clinical as I'd ever seen. I left his room fighting back tears and faking smiles to those walking out of the elevator. I pressed "L" for the lobby, and when the doors shut, I stared at the floor so no one could see my tears flowing to the ground. When the doors opened, I hustled to the garage, again with my face down. I focused on the steps in front of me. I started the car and began crying. I begged God to change him during the next year.

The doctors told him he had to go to a rehab facility. He could go to a great facility closer to his house or to the best of the best, the Rehab Institute of Chicago (RIC), but the latter was farther away. He'd have fewer visitors. Eric said it was the biggest no-brainer ever. He wanted to get better more than he wanted visitors. He'd be going to the RIC.

Most people spend thirty to forty-five days at the RIC for rehab. That's the time improvements max out. Afterward, very little improvement occurs. But Eric was determined. Because of his drive and his continual improvement, Eric spent the next ninety-three days at the RIC.

At the RIC, every time something awesome happened or a major goal was achieved by a patient, a bell would ring. He knew he had to hear that bell rung for his accomplishments. Not for the sake of praise or ego but to get where he wanted to be.

At the RIC, Eric had to learn everything all over again. He had to learn how to get a fork and hold it, how to flip over from his back to his side and back again. He had to learn how to sit up. Sit up? Really? It was so hard. Eric, at six feet and 200-plus pounds was a beast to lift. A hundred-pound female physical therapist helped raise him from his bed. He needed to sit up. As she lifted big E out of bed, he blacked out only to find her lying on top of him. You see, he hadn't been in a standing position since he was in the accident. Again and again he'd be lifted, only to black out again. But his goals. He had goals. He had to try again. A little further each time. He needed to sit up. To move to the next goal, he had to be able to sit up, a full ninety degrees, to the Lokomat, a computer-assisted treadmill.

Anyone on a Lokomat machine looks like a puppet on strings connected to a harness, a kind of life vest. They then attach all kinds of contraptions to every part of the body so it can simulate walking and stimulate muscles. This was Eric's goal. If he could get to ninety degrees, he could get on the Lokomat. Maybe the doctors would be wrong. Maybe he could walk again. Maybe, but ninety degrees stood in his way.

The insurance company would allow him ten sessions unless he showed marked improvement. If he showed marked improvement, he could continue. *Ninety degrees, then the Lokomat, the Lokomat, the Lokomat* was all Eric could think of. Lokomat He pressed on.

Time and time, Eric would try to get to ninety degrees. Blackout. Blackouts would be rewarded with another effort. *Ring.* The bell! He'd done it! The Lokomat! He was so excited. The effort had been worth it. Small things were major victories. He loved hearing that bell.

But ninety degrees wasn't enough, he was told. He had to stay at ninety degrees for thirty minutes. That bell. He needed that bell to get to the Lokomat. That darn bell.

Once he went to the Lokomat, all of the connectors attached to the computer would simulate the walking. Sure, it wasn't his action at first, but Eric was thrilled beyond belief to be able to take basic steps. It had been months since he had walked. Sure, it wasn't like he had in the past, but he was like a proud papa, standing and walking. The Lokomat would teach him how to walk again.

Bells rang again and again for Eric. After his first two times on the Lokomat, Eric was stunned to find that he could actually move his toes and his legs a bit. Without help. The nurse told him there were so many people who wanted to walk out of RIC but very few did. "I can't believe it," she said. "You're the first person we've seen who has had this much progress. It's simply amazing."

During this time, an angel entered his life. Jill Landry became his buddy, his therapist, someone he could bond with and trust. Jill was sent by God to impact Eric. Jill was young, fit, athletic, and strong, strong enough to move Eric. She could help lift him and get him ready for his activities. She had a biting sense of humor that matched Eric's sharp, quick wit. She pushed Eric when he was worn down. She was his RIC angel.

After Eric was discharged, he kept in contact with Jill. The physical aspect of her rehab work took its toll. She ultimately developed back problems due to all the lifting and moved to California to become a chef, but Eric and Joan considered Jill an angel sent by God for that time of his life. The fact that she left physical therapy for a different field was proof she was an angel put on earth for Eric when he needed one the most. With Jill, the bells had rung more frequently.

Eventually, they had Eric stand in braces called KFOs, knee foot orthotics. At first, he stood for three minutes, then five, ten, thirty minutes. Ring, ring. He graduated to AFOs, ankle foot orthotics. Then on to the parallel bars. He stood between them and walked their length and made the return trip. More rings of that bell.

The walker was next. Ring. He was told to walk the halls, and they would measure how far and how fast he walked. He ended up each day exhausted, but ring, ring—more and more victories. His drive, confidence, and determination increased with every ring.

Eric was to do four hours of therapy a day at the RIC, the minimum for every patient. If he wanted more, he could take it whenever he wanted. He'd ask for more therapy. As much as he could get. He'd do seven or eight hours a day. He saw some throw in the towel. He wanted no part of that. Joan was a bastion of strength, and she loved him. Five beautiful kids waited for him. He couldn't get enough therapy.

Eventually, Eric was discharged from inpatient treatment and got to work as an outpatient. For the next year and a half, Eric and Joan commuted two or three times a week for therapy, eschewing a facility only forty-five minutes away for R.I.C., even though R.I.C. was an hour and a half each way. They wanted the best. He wanted to be pushed. He needed his angel. He needed that bell.

Eric finished his therapy in under two years but continued to work out about four hours a day. He decided to return to practice. He practices, although not full time, but he has a long list of patients who love him ... and a much-deserved waiting list.

Things aren't perfect for Eric. I remember Mom asking him if he had his choice, would he choose full dexterity with his hands or being fully mobile with his legs. He said he wanted his legs. He said God had given him what he needed to continue fully participating in life.

I asked Eric what his thoughts were as he went through the process. As a doctor, he said, "I knew I was screwed," when he heard the doctors talking. He was mad. He had gone from his best physical condition to incapacitation. He was mad at the kid who had hit him, and he hated his lot in life.

Just after the accident, all sense of pride started slipping away. Nurses were putting catheters in him daily. They'd see everything. His junk. Nothing was private. He was poked and prodded. It was horrible. He was mad, but he was also scared. But he said that after about ten days, all pride was gone. He didn't care who saw what anymore. He just wanted to get better.

The toughest moment for Eric was one day after therapy. He was doing more than twice the amount of therapy than most patients and was often exhausted. After getting back from his four-hour therapy session one day, he told Joan, "I'm done. I'm working my butt off, and this is all I've progressed. I'm done."

At that moment, another patient came zipping into his room in a wheelchair. He had heard Eric and said, "Life in a wheelchair is great, dude. Look at me. I'm zipping around like nobody's business. Life is good. I press the button this way and I go this way. Or I hit the button this way and I zoom that way. Don't get down, dude. Life is good."

As soon as the wheelchair patient told him life was great in a wheelchair, Eric said to Joan, "Let's go. Time for extra therapy." He wasn't going to live in a wheelchair. Another God moment of motivation. Perfect timing. Suck it up and move forward.

When asked later about his feelings about the guy who had hit him, Eric said he had initially been mad, but he had gotten through it almost immediately. He said if he had focused on the person who had hit him, he wouldn't have been able to focus on what he needed to do to get better. "I'm sure this guy didn't intend to harm me. I'm sure if he had the chance to do it all over again, he wouldn't do it again. I don't even know the name of the guy who hit me. I don't want to know. If he would choose to undo what had been done, why should I be mad at him, someone who never intended to harm me in the first place?" Really? Not even a bit of anger? Amazing. Eric knew,

- If he stayed angry at the other driver, he would never be able to focus on his recovery and his family, and he knew family and recovery were the most important goals.
- The other driver had to carry that burden of what he had done to Eric and his family for the rest of his life.
- The weight of Eric's recovery was tough enough, but if he had to also carry anger about something that couldn't be undone, it would be too much.

Is Eric's life better today? Absolutely. Sure, he'd rather have his legs and feet running marathons, but he said, "Before, I was so consumed with work. With building a great medical practice. I wanted my office to be successful. Most nights, I'd get home around seven. I'd eat, work out, and go to bed. I didn't spend much time with my family. I was spending most of my time trying to provide for them. I was a good dad and a good husband, but I wasn't a great one. Today, Joan and I talk more than ever, about everything under the sun. I'm close with all five kids. I know everything going on in their lives. I often know more about the kids than Joan does. We're a much closer and better family because of this."

Jeremiah 29:11 NEW INTERNATIONAL VERSION tells us, "'For I know the plans I have for you,' declares the LORD, 'plans to prosper you and not to harm you, plans to give you hope and a future.'" Many would say Eric had been harmed, but in truth, Eric looks at his life as a blessing. He's appreciative and grateful for his position in life. Sure, if he could undo what had been done, he would, but today, he is living every second of his life as best as he can, and he appreciates it.

Eric had always been the type of guy who could have a conversation with a wall and the wall would end up feeling good about itself. During his recovery and rehab at the RIC, he found people were drawn to him just as before. Other patients with injuries more severe sought him out.

One young man at the RIC came in with the same injury Eric had experienced only months before. The man had sustained paralysis. He was a young buck. A real lady's man. Eric told him to take advantage of every second of rehab he could. He shared his story, but the guy wouldn't listen. He treated therapy as a joke. He snuck out of the RIC at night with buddies and got drunk. He eventually was kicked out of the RIC for not following the rules. Eric saw him one year later. The guy could move only one toe. The patient asked for the Lokomat. He said he was serious. But it was too late. Lokomat was not an option at that point for him. The time for regaining movement was immediately after the injury. He had wasted his opportunity. No rewinds.

Another man who came in was as depressed as Eric had been when he was admitted. Again, Eric told the man his story but added, "These nurses don't care if you walk again. They're here to do a job. At five o'clock, they go home to their families. Just sitting around here moping and trying to punish everyone because of your injury won't help you. It won't hurt your parents or your friends or the staff. It'll hurt only you. If you want to get better, it'll be because of you. It'll be because of your heart. It'll be because you make it happen."

Within weeks, the man was up and walking the halls. That's impact. Even in the position Eric was in physically and mentally, he could still impact the lives of others. He could make a difference. This man may have come to the same conclusion on his own, but Eric knew he had made a difference. The other man tried to make a difference as well. Eric knew he had done the right thing. Doing the right thing always feels good.

I asked Eric what had changed his outlook. Had there been a defining moment? He said a young Hispanic woman in her early thirties came to the RIC due to viral meningitis. She couldn't move anything from the neck down. She was confined to a wheelchair. To move, she had to blow into a tube once. To stop, she had to blow into the tube twice. To turn left, she had to blow three times. Four times to turn right, and so on. "I kept thinking that she was so screwed," he said, "but every time Joan and I saw her, she would give the most beautiful smile we'd ever seen. It would melt the hardest of hearts. I got to thinking, if she could smile, how could I ever be mad at what's going on in my life?"

I'm not sure everyone would process what had happened and respond as well as Eric did. So many people are waiting for the lottery. They're waiting for someone else to make their lives better. I think of all the crappy marriages I saw during my days as a counselor. Women thought having a husband would make them happy. A new baby would save a marriage. Men thought they needed wives, just like their friends, to complete their lives and achieve happiness. Never could anything be so more wrong. Happiness begins at home. Without happiness at home, there is no way anyone can make someone else happy. Even more tragically, there's no way anyone else can make that person happy.

You need to stand on your own feet. You've been dealt a distinct hand in life. You may think your life, your hand, is crappy, but in truth, you have the cards you need to win the game. Your game. You may have a winning hand but spend too much time peering at others' cards. You can never utilize your gifts if you spend time looking at others' gifts. The odds are that even those who appear happy aren't. Most people aren't. We live in a society of envy instead of appreciation. When you can see your gifts and talents the way God sees them, you will begin to utilize them and start down the path toward happiness.

Sadly, most people will read this and say, "But Larry, you don't know my circumstances." I don't. I'll never know your circumstances, but I don't want to. My circumstances are challenging in their own ways, but I, too, was fortunate to wake up one day and think that I have a pretty good lot in life and that I'm going to make something awesome of it.

With every success comes more confidence. With more confidence comes more success, and the cycle continues. Muscle isn't built without resistance. Astronauts in space lose muscle mass because of having no resistance. NASA has determined astronauts need weight-resistance exercises when in space to maintain muscle. It's the same with you. Resistance and failure are good. Persistence is the best. Persistence all but ensures victory. Too many times, I've seen people quit. Right before victory. They replace the quest for happiness with Friday-night escapes. Friday-night parties can seem to be a good time, but in truth, they're just an excuse to run and hide for a bit. Victory will come to those who persevere. For those who don't, momentary escape is their only pleasure. Our society is leaning further and further this way every year.

In fairness, Eric had a great support system. His parents were bastions of support. His in-laws bent over backward to help with the family's needs. Joan never left his side. Eric had been dealt a good hand. What is significant is that he recognized what he had and decided to play it.

Joan remembers the whole situation as brutal. She recollects the call from my father. Once she realized he wasn't kidding about the accident, she was off to the races. She got the kids placed elsewhere and ran down to the hospital. Just seeing Eric gave her a sense of relief. She said there really wasn't time for emotion. Just action. Eric needed her. The kids needed her. She needed to be strong. The conversations with Eric weren't going to be about feelings but about actions and goals. The toughest part would be her inability to control the situation as she did in other aspects of her life. Others were in control, and that sucked.

After the accident came a lawsuit. Eric had five kids and a wife to provide for, but he didn't want to drag any suit on. Despite his attorney's recommendation, Eric wanted the case resolved quickly. He wanted to move on with his life. Lengthy litigation would prevent that. If it went to trial, he'd have to confront the man who had hit him. He didn't want that.

The attorney assured Eric that if he stood by his guns, he could get triple what was being offered in the settlement. Eric said, "I just want it to be done. I need to be a dad. I need to be a dad who works. Even though I quit getting disability if I go back to work, I need to work. My kids need to see a dad who works." He settled quickly so he could get on with his life.

Eric models behavior to his kids. A dad sitting on a couch and living off a fat settlement is a dad telling his kids work has no value. He wasn't going to ruin his kids.

Buy a man a fish and you'll feed him for a day. Teach a man to fish and you'll feed him for a life. This was a driving factor in being the parent he was called to be. Sure, he needed money because of the injuries. After all, he is classified as an incomplete quadriplegic,C-6, c-7. Asia B. Moved to Asia C, and then to D. He needed money for his kids' education. But he wasn't looking for a get-rich-quick, big, fat home run. He just wanted to get back on the playing field.

Eric fought. He still fights today. He walks a number of miles a day with one or two of his children. Some people without injuries won't walk to the end of their driveways, much less a mile. He walk is labored but purposed.

You too have your purpose. You know your goal. You see what the end results could be. If you quit, you'll never get to where you need to be. But you won't quit. There's no one ringing that bell for you, but you can hear it with each victory. The obstacles thrown in front of you are brutal. They're real. But you will fight through them. Ring, ring, ring. You're breaking your goal down to a lot of steps. Each step is a bell. What's your reward? For Eric, the bell was enough reward. For you, your reward may be a night out on the town. It may be a weekend away. But each step of achievement results in a ring of your personal bell.

Some guy in a wheelchair will zip on up and say, "Why bother working so hard? Life in this wheelchair isn't all that bad. Look at me." But your goal is so much greater than that. You'll have none of it. You want the bell. You need the bell. To get to your goal, you'll need to take a step and hear a bell. Take another step and hear another bell. Until you've reached your goal.

JOSETTE: LOVE

Love

If I speak in the tongues of men or of angels, but do not have love, I am only a resounding gong or a clanging cymbal. If I have the gift of prophecy and can fathom all mysteries and all knowledge, and if I have a faith that can move mountains, but do not have love, I am nothing. If I give all I possess to the poor and give over my body to hardship that I may boast, but do not have love, I gain nothing.

Love is patient, love is kind. It does not envy, it does not boast, it is not proud. It does not dishonor others, it is not self-seeking, it is not easily angered, it keeps no record of wrongs. Love does not delight in evil but rejoices with the truth. It always protects, always trusts, always hopes, always perseveres.

Love never fails. But where there are prophecies, they will cease; where there are tongues, they will be stilled; where there is knowledge, it will pass away. For we know in part and we prophesy in part, but when completeness comes, what is in part disappears. When I was a child, I talked like a child, I thought like a child, I reasoned like a child. When I became a man, I put the ways of childhood behind me. For now we see only a reflection

as in a mirror; then we shall see face to face. Now I know
in part; then I shall know fully, even as I am fully known.

And now these three remain: faith, hope and love. But
the greatest of these is love. (1 Corinthians 13) NEW
INTERNATIONAL VERSION

Sometimes, an angel comes into your life and you don't even know it.

I'm not really sure how Josette and I came to be friends. We worked at
the same company. I was in Illinois and she was in Colorado. Josette had
joined the company a few months prior to my joining, but since she had
come before me, I thought she had been there for years.

I'd see her at company functions. She was polite, kind, and courteous.
For practical matters, she was not the type of gal I would want to hang
out with. Nothing bad about her at all, but unlike me, she was polished,
reserved, focused, and professional. On the other hand, I, with my very
short attention span, had to be constantly moving, seeking action and
excitement. Polished professionals bored me. I wanted someone to rock
the boat, keep me on my toes, and keep life interesting. Josette wasn't
that person. She was focused.

I traveled to Colorado for corporate functions and events at least three or
four times a year. I'd spend at least a day driving from Denver to Rocky
Mountain National Park or Boulder and hang with old friends. After a day
of meetings and conferences, I wanted to be alone to clear the crap that
had accumulated over a day of travel, work on my projects, or go out at
night to let my hair down with my coworkers. Josette wasn't going out
at night to party, so we rarely had the opportunity to spend significant
time with each other except at company functions.

Still, over the course of the years, we would talk. As I got to know Josette
better, I learned she had a sly and quick wit, a quiet sense of humor, and

a tongue as sharp as mine. *How attractive,* I thought as I got to know her better. Maybe there was more under her hood than I had thought. She was Irish Catholic, and I was German-Irish Catholic. When she let me know she had grown up loving Notre Dame and Notre Dame football, I realized I had missed years with her because of my preconceived notions.

Conversations of Notre Dame led to Lou Holtz, football, family history, faith, and leadership. Although our conversations were sincere, they were mostly surface and a bit superficial. No feelings. No fears. No dreams or aspirations. Conversations revolved around fun, Notre Dame, our offices, our employees, and leadership challenges. Still, a level of trust grew between us.

Over the last few years, we spoke more and more. When conferences came, we sought each other out. We were now grizzled veterans of our company. Our bonding became deeper. My gut told me there was something more in our relationship, but I didn't know what or why. You know the feeling when your gut just tells you this person is the real deal. I had that with Josette.

I'd share with Josette what was going on with my family, and I'd share my stories with Michelle and my family after I got home. Josette never married for reasons I only later understood. She was a prime catch. Plus, I'd reason, as an Irish Catholic, it was her moral duty to get married and have a million kids.

Josette did love kids, so it really shouldn't have surprised me when she started sending care packages to our five kids over Christmas or Valentine's Day or for other special events. Josette and my middle daughter, Claire, found mutual affection for each other. At the tender age of eight, Claire would send letters and hand-drawn pictures to Josette that would end up in Josette's office. Every night, our family would mention Josette in our prayer list, but she remained at the forefront of Claire's heart and prayers.

Sometimes an angel comes into your life and you don't even know it.

On May 27, 2011, at 2:00 p.m. exactly, Josette got the news. She hadn't been feeling well for quite some time. She didn't feel sick, but she didn't feel well either. She knew physically she was out of sorts. Things didn't seem right. She had some nagging pains in her stomach area that just wouldn't go away.

For a while, Josette rationalized the pain. Up to that day in May, our mortgage industry had been going through some major changes and overhauls. For seasoned veterans such as Josette and me, it was a frustrating time. More government regulations. More government rules. More documents. More compliance. Less client interaction. It was a perfect storm. Josette was sure that popping an antacid or two would alleviate the pain in her stomach caused by an industry run amuck. But the pain, though dull, was beginning to annoy her.

Tough it out, she'd tell herself. And Josette was tough. From Pueblo, Colorado, she was the youngest of three children in a second-generation Irish-American family. Her mom had worked at the Pueblo army depot, and her dad had worked as a construction foreman for American Telephone and Telegraph. They met through their avid work in support of the war efforts during World War II. Her parents were true American patriots. She remembers her father saying "Go with God" every time one of the kids walked out the door. She'd claim that phrase as her own and say it to family, friends, and acquaintances.

Her two older brothers reeked with over-the-top intelligence. Her one brother became a priest and obtained a PhD in Rome. The other brother obtained a PhD in fluid dynamics and travels the world creating goodwill by helping nations deal with tsunamis.

With parents as great examples as well as two incredibly successful siblings, it's no wonder Josette graduated from Colorado State with a degree in biochemistry and microbiology. She immediately went into her field of specialty working for major corporations, including Pepsico and Upjohn.

One day during her early years of employment, she was sitting at the intersection on 225 and Parker Road in Denver. A huge truck barreled through the intersection and all but crushed Josette's car. Although she wasn't critically injured, it took her six months to fully recover.

Josette had two choices. She could sit around and milk every second she didn't have to work, or she could be productive. She had always had a passion for real estate, so during those six months, she studied for and obtained a real estate license. Although she had off-the-charts intelligence, she knew her career was not as satisfying as it could be. Josette loved people. She loved interaction. She loved smoothing out things for others, but her career didn't allow for a lot of personal interaction. A choice had to be made. It was obvious. Josette left her corporate job to pursue her love for people in real estate.

As a real estate agent, she spent as much time getting her clients prepped for buying as she did in showing them houses, so she made another leap into the mortgage industry. "MB for microbiology had become MB for mortgage banking," she would explain to others. Quite the leap for Josette, but it all started making sense to her. She could use her brains, and she could help others. She was living the dream.

Over the last twenty years, Josette became a preeminent mortgage banker not only in the Denver area but also in all Colorado. But here she was on May 27, 2011, waiting to see why her pain was not going away. She knew the industry had changed and understood the effects of stress on the body, but why did she still have the pain even three weeks later? It was driving her nuts.

May 27 that year was the Friday before the Memorial Day weekend and the last day to fund real estate closings for May. Josette knew Friday would be busy. She had a doctor's appointment at 10:30 a.m. That meant she had to get to work early.

After taking care of some business in the morning, she went to her appointment. The technician asked her many questions about pain and discomfort. Josette read the seriousness in the tech's voice. It was odd, Josette thought, that she was told to lie down and wait for the radiologist to see if it was okay for Josette to leave.

The tech came back and asked Josette to wait in the lobby while the radiologist ordered additional tests. Josette asked the tech what was going on, but the tech refused to share anything with Josette. *Weird, but following protocol*, Josette thought, trying to convince herself everything would be okay.

Josette had a CT scan. She was told that it'd be about two hours. They gave her some concoction to drink prior to the scan. She drank the foreign liquid and headed to her car to email her office. It was a holiday Friday, so she told them she wasn't going to return but start her weekend a bit early.

She grabbed her rosary and began to pray while she waited. She called her primary care physician at 2:00 p.m. She wanted the results. Josette wasn't willing to waste an entire weekend worrying. She wasn't that type. The person who answered went looking for the doctor. As Josette waited, she could hear scattered conversations among the support staff and nurses as they scrambled to find the doctor.

The physician picked up the phone and said that it was not the type of results he could give over the phone. "It would be unfair to you, Josette," he told her as compassionately as he could. *Give it to me straight, Doc,* was what she was thinking, but she said, "I don't want to go into the weekend without knowing the results. Can you tell me the problem?" she asked politely yet firmly. The doctor said, "You have stage four pancreatic cancer … and yes … it's terminal. There's nothing further we can do for you. You have two to three weeks at best to live."

Conception, birth, playground, friends, grade school, high school, college, work, friends, boyfriends, family, clients, family, friends, family. A life that had impacted the world for more than fifty years was supposed to end in three weeks or less. Although not communicated to her this way, the doctor had basically said, "You will cease to exist in the next three weeks. Have a nice day, and yes, insurance will cover about 80 percent of your medical expenses."

Stunned, she had nothing to say in response. She knew something was up, but stage four pancreatic cancer? As well read as Josette was, she hadn't read the manual on how to respond to such news. Cancer stages take into account the size of the tumor, how much it has spread, and whether it has spread to other organs. The prognosis is never good for stage four pancreatic cancer. He talked to her about options that included chemotherapy and other treatments. He wanted her to see an oncologist at 4:00 that afternoon.

She thanked the doctor and hung up. Staring blankly for a minute, she got into her car, locked the doors, and put on her seatbelt. She had to get to that oncologist. Her head was spinning. *This can't be right*, she thought. There had to be a second opinion.

She called a great friend of hers and her oldest brother. The news was devastating to her brothers. She called others but kept getting voice mails.

On the way to the oncologist, she thought, *God, I don't have the strength or energy for this. I need to just put one foot in front of the other. I have to see this oncologist. It's just not right. I feel great physically, except for a bit of isolated pain.*

The oncologist confirmed her nightmare. He told her that she had few weeks at best to live but that they would put her on an aggressive pain management plan to keep her as comfortable as possible.

Sometimes, an angel comes into your life and you don't even know it.

On her way home, she decided to resign her position as a vice president of her company so she wouldn't be a distraction to the mission she and her employer had envisioned. She called her corporate offices and spoke to Nicole Dillon and asked if she'd be kind enough to have her boss, Stacey Harding, call her.

Stacey loves people. He loves impacting the lives of others. And he loves golf. Nicole couldn't reach Stacey. He was golfing with some clients. His assistant called Stacey and said, "It's important that you call Josette as she had something important to share with you." After finishing his round on the golf course, he called her.

JOSETTE. This is Josette.

STACEY. Hi, Josette, Stacey here. I just received your message. How are you doing, my friend?

JOSETTE. Thanks for calling back. You know, I haven't been feeling up to snuff over the last few weeks, so I went to the doctor. They ran a battery of tests. I got the results, and they're not good.

STACEY. And?

JOSETTE. And, well, I don't know how else to tell you this, but I have been diagnosed with stage four pancreatic cancer.

STACEY. No. Are you serious?

JOSETTE. Unfortunately I am.

STACEY. Wow. I don't know what to say. Are you going to get a second opinion?

JOSETTE. I think I should, but in the meantime, I'm going to tender my resignation. I don't want to be a distraction to my office or to the mission we're all on. I'm going to resign quietly and move on with the next stage of my life. I thought I'd let you know so you can start working on a replacement.

STACEY. Certainly not. I refuse to accept your resignation. Josette, you're going to fight this with everything you have. And I mean everything. Josette, you're going to fight.

The conversation went on for some time about her options and her prognosis. Stacey asked, "Josette you're going to fight, aren't you?" It was then that Josette made a decision she couldn't make for herself earlier. She decided it was indeed time to fight. She would fight with every fiber of muscle in her body. No matter how good or how bad things got, she would fight.

Up until that moment, she had been confused. She had been blindsided by something so heavy and so new that although she was going to get a second opinion, she had already accepted the doctor's prognosis of having only weeks to live. But Stacey had stepped up and helped her find the direction she desperately needed.

Stacey wrapped the conversation up with, "Josette, can I pray for you?" And pray he did. He prayed from his heart. He prayed with Josette straight to the throne of God. They knew God had heard their prayers. Josette's future was mapped out and sealed with a prayer. She would fight more than she had ever fought for anything.

Stacey later told me there are times in life you feel the Holy Spirit coming down and leading everything. Stacey had been through a similar situation just two years prior. His stepmother had been diagnosed with breast cancer and had been told she had only two weeks to live. Stacey had also told her to fight. "Four years later, she's as strong as ever," Stacey said. "I was prepped for this moment with Josette because of what I'd gone through with my stepmom. God prepped me ahead of time for this moment. I just knew."

Sometimes an angel inspires another angel.

Josette slept well that Friday night, although at that time, she really didn't know why she felt such peace. Still, she had just been run over by a train and couldn't focus on her normal weekend activities. She knew she had to get her affairs in order while seeking a second opinion. *Weeks? I have a lot to do*, she'd think. She spent the weekend cleaning her house. She threw away junk. She called people she felt she had wronged in the past and asked for forgiveness. "I didn't want to be a burden on anyone, so I wanted to have everything prepped for everyone for when I died." But still, everything was so overwhelming. It was too fresh. Too new. How could she digest it all? It's just too much to take in. *Just keep busy*, she'd think as she packed another bag and made another call.

The following Monday, she spoke to the president of the company, Jeff May. The conversation was similar to the one she had had with Stacey on Friday. Though she was told she had less than two months to live, Josette wasn't offering her resignation. She let him know her time would be fully committed to the company in between her fights against this disease. Jeff told Josette he loved her and encouraged her in her fight. He reiterated much of what Stacey had said and said, "Josette, we got your back." Every shred of doubt had left Josette. She was committed to the fight.

She wasn't sure what to do. She hadn't been through this before. What she needed was great leadership. A friendly kick in the butt to snap her out of the spell cancer had put her under. The bubble popped. Her mind focused at the task at hand.

Josette sought other medical opinions. She reached out to a doctor in the Midwest who used to practice in her area. She needed some sage advice from within the medical field. She wanted someone who was independent of her as a patient. She gave the doctor the test results, medical records, and patient charts. They conversed for a long time over the phone. He assured her she was doing the right thing by seeking a second opinion. He told her who she should see. He told her something that further inspired her to fight: "Don't let any doctor tell you when your time is up. That's between you and God. No one else knows that time. Go ahead and fight. If it were me, I would."

Sometimes an angel inspires another angel.

Her two months became two years. She became a model patient. The doctors and nurses loved when Josette came in for treatments. She had moved on to clinical trials, and the chemo and other medicine was doing well for her. Her markers looked good, and she felt great.

When arriving for chemo, she became like Norm walking in the bar in the television series *Cheers*. Every time she came through the doors for chemo, everyone would yell, "Josette!"

In a place of death and dying, she became a beacon of light. The doctors and nurses knew that with her cheery, positive, and fighting attitude, she had to become a patient advocate. And did she ever. She became more than an advocate. She became God's angel.

Kind of funny how God works. Just that prior September, she had told God she wanted to make a massive change in her life. She had told God she wanted to impact others in a way she never had before. Josette had influenced others and had had such a positive impact on their lives, but during that prayer, she asked to be God's tool. She wanted to be the hammer God used to construct something great. She wanted to influence others and change lives for the better. For Him. She prayed that day, saying, "God, use me."

She became the de facto mayor of the chemo floor. Her bright and cheerful smile and attitude pierced the hearts of those with similar diagnoses. It was her decision to love. This decision required a lot of work. I think that's why most people won't make this decision. It's just too hard to make a decision to love intentionally all the time. But she received more than she ever gave. And she gave a lot.

She needed her chemo, but she knew she was there to make an impact. Patients came to the floor paralyzed with fear, just as she had been. She'd smile and spend time with them. She'd give hugs and tell them her story of hope. Some receive what she had to offer. Others didn't. It didn't matter. She wasn't doing this for herself. She was doing this for God. She chose to love. Her impact came through her conscious decision to love. Josette was God's employee, His ambassador, His worker. She knew it. God knew it. "Go with God," she'd tell people.

In the elevator on the way up to chemo, she'd pray, "God, show me the people you want to me reach out to today. Give me the words and your Spirit to make an impact. Give me a word of encouragement. Use me to change their lives. I'm yours today. No matter what happens today, it's all about You, not me." The choice. The decision to love.

The elevator door would open, and she would head to the ministry God had called her to. Josette said it was a way for her to channel her own fear. The fear was there, but by focusing on her mission, God's mission, and her purpose, the fear would atrophy and all but disappear during her time on the floor. She had to love. There would be no peace for Josette without love, but it went beyond peace. It went to something deeper for Josette. An eternal fulfillment became lodged in her soul.

Up until the diagnosis, Josette had had a great life. One pivotal moment, she realized she had to give more than she received. When her mom was dying, it was Josette, the thirty-nine year old youngest sibling, who took her off life support. "I was there for her last breath," she would say. "That really changed me. I got to hold her hand as she took her last breath. Mom was there when I was born, and I was there when she died. I had always believed in God, but that moment tied me to Jesus Christ and to life."

From that moment on, she knew that to live she had to serve Christ and others. "I knew God was in that room. It was earthshaking. God moved me to the core of my being."

So there she was on the chemo floor affecting the lives of others. "I don't see the world the same as I used to. I don't see the world the same as others do. I live in the world of the terminally ill cancer patients, and if I have the ability to make their lives better, I know that it's really not me, but God. And that's when I find my happiness." It's that choice. That choice to love.

She'd find a way to lift patients up. Sometimes it was cookies she made for the staff. Sometimes it was hugs she would give to cancer patients crying and in fear, knowing life would never be the same. She'd always say, "Be sure to travel with God in your heart," as a parting shot to patients. She didn't care about religion. She wanted each person to know that God was real, that God was there and ready to meet them exactly where they were at that moment.

One time, a woman was crying because she was losing her hair. She had been a beautiful woman, but the chemo had taken her hair faster than any barber could have. Josette saw the woman and knew it was time. Wigs cost thousands, and the woman losing her hair cried, telling the nurse she had barely enough to get by much less for a luxury like a thousand-dollar wig. Josette gently removed her wig and, with a smile, handed it to the patient. "Be sure to travel with God in your heart." She walked back to her table to continue her own treatments. Her decision to love paid immediate dividends.

Sometimes, an angel comes into your life, and you finally know it.

She had told God she wanted to be used by Him to positively impact others. In complete irony, through her own battle with cancer, Josette was doing just that. And she was doing it better than she ever had. The cancer patients knew she had street cred. She was one of them. They knew she knew what she was talking about. She became the world's greatest player coach.

She said that often, she needed about three people to carry all the stuff she brought into the hospital. Sure, she had to bring in things for the doctor, but she also had to bring in gifts for the patients she'd see any one day. She would give crosses made of palm branches each day to whomever she encountered. She would make a point to remember just one thing about each person she met so she could find a way to connect with him or her. To elicit a smile that had been hidden in their heart. That decision to love.

"I had free reign on the floor. I would just roam from room to room. It made me feel so good. Sometimes, I'd just bring them their favorite Starbuck's coffee. It seemed as if I handed out a zillion copies of the book *Fifty Days of Hope* to anyone who wanted hope."

For those who didn't want hope, she would give them a copy anyway. How could anyone say no? "You get to know people really well when you have eight hours of chemo treatments. It was like an entirely different social scene. I loved it," she'd say.

When the traditional chemo quit working for Josette, she had a break in chemo and moved to clinical trials with a new chemo regimen. During this time, she was called to testify before Congress, asking for more money for research for pancreatic cancer. Being off of cancer-fighting medication while the body cleanses itself of prior treatment cycles doesn't make a lot of sense to anyone outside of oncology. It would seem to me that not having the drugs would allow cancer to further metastasize. It may, but it may be enough of a cleanse so the next cancer-fighting regimen has a fighting chance.

Josette is a fighter. As of this moment, she is still fighting. The doctors tell her that the clinical trials are no longer working and that she needs to cleanse her body for another thirty days before moving on to other experimental treatments. The medicine has wreaked havoc on her body. But she believes there is a tomorrow for her. "Christ died so we could live," she'd say. "If I accepted what the doctors had said, I would have wasted every day waiting. I would have missed two and a half years of every days. I'm living every day as if I have something to live for."

Her cancer is being managed as best as can be expected. Only her inner circle will hear that Josette has to crawl from her kitchen to her bedroom when the pain becomes too much. She shares these facts with so few, but more as a matter of fact rather than an indictment of her lot in life. If the pain forces her to cry, she doesn't share that with anyone. It's not to put on a brave front. Every day is a gift, and whining to others instead of helping others would seem ungrateful. And Josette is grateful for every day.

When it comes to legacy, Josette made it clear. "I try to be Christlike. I want people to see and know compassion. I never expect anything in return. After all, for all of us, it's just between us and Christ anyway. Can I treat others well regardless of how they treated me? Even before cancer, I never wanted to go out mad and angry. I guess I want people to know they need to live with joy no matter what life offers. The best days are always ahead." That decision to love.

She hasn't beaten the cancer yet, but the cancer hasn't beaten her either. She still holds her position at work, often putting in long hours to serve her clients. Josette has to be working with people. She meets with more senators and congressmen to find more funding to defeat cancer. She has her stash of gifts all set for the next visit to the chemo floor. Unwitting nurses, doctors, and patients will soon have brushes with love.

I was blind cc'd on an email she sent to her entire office:

> First of all, thank you for your patience the last three weeks as I had to travel so much to meet with some of the best oncologists in the country to determine best options for treatment. I have decided on a treatment plan with MD Anderson and the treatment plan is what they call "off-label," not a trial, but not an approved regimen for pancreatic cancer but used in other cancers.
>
> I will have to travel to MD Anderson once per month for what they call hepatic arterial infusion (HAI) of a chemo drug that does require I admit to the hospital for the two-day infusion … the second chemo drug is given every two weeks, but I will be in Denver and that is a normal chemo IV and delivery … I will be reunited with my chemo team in Denver!
>
> Amazing but insurance approved the entire protocol (thank you, Jeff May, for our benefits!)—this protocol because it is "off label" requires your insurance company to pay for, so imagine having treatments approved at two different cancer centers with two oncologists involved, two chemo teams, just to make the patient's life a bit easier … very blessed.

Certainly there are no guarantees and not a cure but this regimen may control the disease to allow more time, very new in studies ... it is new to the pancreatic world (only a handful of PC patients are receiving) so I am hoping this can buy more time and maybe provide an option for other PC patients! Or perhaps become part of a normal regimen and many more patients will benefit as insurance companies start to accept this as an option to very stubborn cancers ... currently only a few research centers are allowed to deliver chemo with this method and I am blessed to have this chance.

When I left Monday afternoon for Houston, I had not heard if we had insurance approval and knew it was still pending and had been bumped up to review—I had to decide whether I get on that plane and take a leap of faith or give up my appt and reschedule for two to three weeks—so today as I was on the shuttle to MD Anderson an email came thru letting me know that insurance had approved the HAI procedure and would also allow me to receive my additional chemo in Denver under Dr. Feiner.

So later this evening I will admit to the hospital and for the next two days I will have a private room with TV and nothing to do but hear from you all and try and help where I can.

The first book I read after being diagnosed was *When God and Cancer Meet*. I can tell you that my journey has been just that, so,

Support the fighters
Admire the survivors

Honor the taken
And never ever give up hope!

God Bless!

Josette

PS: please do not hesitate to ask for my help or cc me on
an email. You are all a part of the healing process and I
love you all!

Josette took her flight in faith, believing God would have the insurance
company approve the procedure. She didn't know prior to the flight. She
didn't know after the flight. But she took the one available slot, believing
God was greater than her situation. As she arrived at the hospital, she
received word the insurance company had approved the procedure. And
so she continues.

Hope keeps her going. Love fuels her focus. By focusing on the needs of
others, she rarely has time for worry or fear. Sure, it's there, but it won't
consume her as long as she's sharing her love with others.

When you realize you have an angel in your life, you never want her to
leave.

Josette knows her task. She has to get better. To fight with all she has.
She also knows that to make her mark in the world, she needs to use the
DNA God gave her to impact the lives of those she comes in contact with.

As of the printing of this book, Josette has had many positive changes and
her diagnosis has improved markedly. She's gone from a poor diagnosis to
one where hope for a long healthy life exists. That doesn't mean that she
is cured, but it does mean that where no hope existed, hope now abounds.

You may have tragedies or hardships. Are they there to take your focus away from what you have been called to do, or can you focus on what you have been called to do? What would you do? Would your final blast in life be to accept what a doctor tells you? Would you accept the negative report someone hands you? Would you respond with anger and withdraw while sitting on the sideline waiting for death?

You have a goal only you can achieve. No one else was called to do what you've been called to do. You step up and pursue what's in your heart or you don't. You know what you've been called to do. It's never left you. It's in your heart. Perhaps deep, but it's there. As Josette learned, without love, life is empty and meaningless.

Josette is living a fuller life in battling cancer than most healthy people ever will. Most people aren't truly living. Most aren't truly serving. Most aren't truly loving. As a result, they're living empty, meaningless lives. What's beautiful, however, is that yesterday does not matter. It's just yesterday. It doesn't define your today or tomorrow.

While Josette by all practical measures has had a very successful life, she wanted to make a larger, more impactful difference. God places people where He wants them. She had angels placed in her life along the way to guide her.

Can you be that angel to someone else? Can you find the opportunity where you are today to make a difference in the life of someone else? It doesn't matter how that person responds. Josette said it best: "It was never between you and them anyway. It was always between you and God."

When you realize that you have an angel in your life, you never want her to leave.

"And now these three remain: faith, hope and love. But the greatest of these is love" (1 Corinthians 13:13). NEW INTERNATIONAL VERSION

LIFE PLANNING

Take me back in time, let me fill my mind with the memory
Of the place I stood when I felt my dreams could carry me
With my words and my plan and my heart in my hands, I was ready then
When the doubters came I would keep my aim, In spite of them
But these days sometimes I feel so uninspired
Till I close my eyes and remember what I'm living for

I'm not lost anymore
I'm driven by the deeper why
I can change the world
'Cause I took the time
And I know the reason why

I can find myself in this busy place pushing to succeed
The commotion can cloud all the focus I have right in front of me
The daily grind gets me down sometimes, but still I know
All these changing lanes, they can't rearrange where I'm want to go
These days sometimes I feel so uninspired
So I close my eyes and call to mind what I'm living for

I'm not lost anymore
I'm driven by the deeper why
I can change the world
'Cause I took the time
To I know the reason why

Gonna start a revolution here and now
Feel my existence, make a difference somehow

I'm not lost anymore
I am driven by the deeper why
I can change the world
I took the time
And I know the reason why

"The Deeper Why" by Justin Sheehy, © 2010 Sheehy Songs

Public service announcement. Go to I Tunes and download this song by Justin Sheehy. It's a great song and it keep you focused on the "deeper why" in your life.

Mary, a wonderful woman, has a great job with a marketing company. Ten years ago, she became national vice-president. She's well-liked and respected among her peers and employees. She has one child in college and another in high school. Her husband is well respected in the community, and they have a good marriage. Every day on her way home, she stops at a local convenience store and buys a couple of lottery tickets, hoping for that one big hit. Although she's at the top at her company, it's been the same for the last ten years. There's nowhere higher to go.

She always wanted her own marketing company. She has so many great ideas. Her company loves her and her ideas, but she imagines how much bigger they could be if she were the kingpin. As a prisoner of her own mind, Mary has convinced herself she cannot leave. How could she leave her salary and benefits? Plus, her three bosses treat her so darn well. She'd feel guilty leaving them. She's not miserable with her life and career, but she hopes that one lotto ticket would allow her to walk away and start up Mary's Marketing, Inc.

Joe is different. He works his butt off, but he has accepted the same routine life gives him. He works for a hospital and has great benefits. He has a loving wife and kids, but in truth, he doesn't realize he's mired in the same routine. He works long hours. He attends all his kids' activities. He loves them dearly but is drowning in his routine. Early to rise and the last to bed. His one outlet is hitting the bar on the way home on Fridays with his buddies. He's not an alcoholic. Just a couple of drinks once a week to unwind. It's been that way for years. He meets his buddies at a pub to get a couple of beers, his treat to himself. Just a little solo time to decompress. He once had a great vision for he and his wife. He was going to learn his trade. After perfecting it, he's be a consultant and dictate his own wages and his own hours. He would spend more time with his family and use the extra income for vacations, child education and retirement. But the vision he had has been lost through work and wife and kids.

While living lives most would consider successful, Mary and Joe are living uninspiring and, quite frankly, unfulfilling lives. Mary wanted something more, but when she achieved her goal, she let go of her dream to open her own company. *A bit of safety*, she rationalized to herself.

Joe has a nice life, but he's lost his passion. He rarely gets free time, and when he does, it's usually on Friday nights. Joe is trapped in the routine and has walked away from his larger dream. He blames it on his stage in life.

I haven't thrown in the wife married to a cheating husband. I haven't thrown in a husband who lost his kids through divorce or the parents who lost their son to suicide. Joe and Mary are the successful ones, yet in their hearts, they have kept their passions buried.

The problem is that most don't know their passions or they have lost them. If a passion is known, the second question must be, Why is that passion so important? Justin Sheehy's song "The Deeper Why" talks about the reasons why. If you can understand your passion and the reason why, you just need a plan. This is where the concept of life planning becomes critical.

For most of us, life just happens. Same job. Same routine. Sure, we mix it up here and there. New jobs, new vacations, and new goals come and go, but the overall plan hasn't changed. We fill ourselves up with treats since we work so hard. But we're missing more. We're missing passion. Getting that job was great, but now what? Same with marriage, parenting, buying a home, or whatever. Often, we're left with the question, now what?

Wendy and Eric made a decision to change their lives as a reaction to something powerful. All at once, their eyes opened up. Each saw a bigger picture, but in truth, each was responding to an event. Your passion can often be buried so deep that you have no clue it's there. Once it's uncovered, it's almost impossible to bury again.

Michael Jordan had the big picture. He had an outrageous dream to become the best at every level he played. From high school through the NBA, he coupled his vision with an incredible work ethic and a very narrow, precise plan. In high school, his goal wasn't to be the best player in NBA history but just to make the team. Every year, he redefined his goal until he retired as the greatest ever. Did he create a life plan? No, and maybe, as a result, other areas in his life suffered. The focus on his passion paid off, but what about the other passions?

David faltered because he forgot his reason why. He forgot his passion. He sought the pleasure of the moment when he sacrificed the complete inner fulfillment of achieving his mission.

Josette had a plan. She had been life planning for years. Just six months prior to her cancer diagnosis, she had updated her life plan. Amending it that year, she asked God to allow her to make a major impact on the lives of others. Her plan was in place. When it came time to react, she did so in ways consistent with her updated life plan.

Most people don't have a clear life plan for their lives. If a plan occurs, it's as a result of suddenly seeing the opportunity that lies before them coupled with truly understanding the gifts and talents in their arsenals. Few people understand this life is not a dry run. There are no rewinds. Yesterday doesn't matter except to learn from.

If you fail to plan, you plan to fail. Most people don't plan their lives at all. People will tell you they do, but rarely do they. Maybe they've thought their lives out, but even that's rare. They always think about what they wanted their lives to be, but other than going to college and getting degrees and jobs and getting married, they never had a life plan. What's the big picture? Graduating from college and getting married are important but momentary milestones—isolated events. Life becomes reactive instead of proactive. Momentary instead of perpetual. Every day should be a fulfilling step in a quest that stirs your heart. Otherwise, each day becomes another in a routine life that can be very safe but very unfulfilling. No direction. No purpose. A sailboat without a rudder will go wherever the waves push it.

No rewind! One shot. Life is too short. All that you have is your now and any tomorrow God gives you. In his book *No Easy Day*, Mark Owen writes that the motto of the Navy SEALs is, "The only easy day is yesterday." Your past is your past. Change is hard, but the rewards are beyond anything you could fathom. But to say you'll change without a plan is highly unlikely. Without a plan, your yesterday becomes your tomorrow.

I hope you understand this next takeaway. It's huge. It's monstrous. It's over the top. You need to get it in the core of your being.

Everyone Pays!

You can pursue your dreams and the costs associated with it, or you can move on with what you currently have and hope for change. Either way you pay. If you decide to pursue your passion, you will need a plan to achieve it. The plan won't be written overnight. It may take you days or weeks to create it, but for a goal or a dream as big as yours, you will need to invest time in making sure you can achieve it. There will be a cost. It may be money. It may be time. It may be time away from things you enjoy or things that comfort you. It may just be lack of sleep as you put your plan in motion. You have to decide if the things you'll give up are worth the results if you achieve you goal. But if you had the ability to achieve your BHAG (big hairy audacious goals) in life, wouldn't it be worth a day or two on working on the passion, the why, and the plan?

My father is a well-respected anesthesiologist who recently retired. He once told me that you never see any fat elderly people. "Why?" I asked. "Because they all die before they turn old. Health-related complications. Their body can't handle the weight." He told me that for every five pounds a person is overweight, the body has one extra mile of blood vessels to pump blood through. That increases blood pressure. If you lose five pounds, you retract that mile.

There's a price every person pays in every facet of life. The guy who maintains his health pays up-front for a longer, better, and healthier life. The guy who can't pass up another snack or another killer will also pay, sooner or later, with health issues or a premature death. Actually, everyone pays. The critical question is, will you decide when you'll pay, or will a payment be forced upon you? If you don't choose to pay up-front, the consequences may be beyond anything you ever fathomed. As my dad said, "You don't want to be lucky to be in rehab. The ones in rehab from a heart attack are the lucky ones. The ones who die aren't so much."

When it comes to health, if I know I'm going to pay, I'd rather pay on my terms. I'd rather pay up-front instead of being hopeful I'll be in rehab someday down the road.

Same with the guy who likes to drink. Same with the person who likes to party. Same with the married person who wants a social life outside of marriage. I've known so many men and women who were married but acted as if they weren't. They hit the town, leaving their spouse alone or with the kids while they lived a free lifestyle. Many act as if a ceremony and a marriage certificate validates the marriage. It doesn't, and, as a result, so many marriages are in shambles today. Real men and women embrace their commitments to marriage. They pay the price up-front. They grow up and learn their responsibilities as spouses. By embracing the cost up-front, the payoff is in the long run with a good marriage and a good family. Those who refuse to commit to their marriage vows up-front end up paying later. They see counselors in therapy or pay divorce lawyers.

I watched a story about some young, intelligent guy with a great job who had date-raped many women over a seven-year period. He was good looking, charming, well educated, and well spoken. The judge gave him life imprisonment. This guy, barely thirty, chose to pay for some fun up-front with a life sentence. He took from others thinking he wouldn't pay with the rest of his life. Everyone pays.

When will you pay? The choice is 100 percent yours. It's all yours. It belongs to no one else. Whether you want that power or not, it belongs to you. Your friends can't make your decision for you. Only you can. Will you invest a day or two in yourself to ensure the rest of your life is all you hoped it would be? Or will you live for immediate pleasures and pay for the rest of your life? Will you roll the dice and see what you can get away with? Wisdom says pay today.

By creating my life plan, I greatly increased my odds of success through true clarity. If you combine true clarity with passion, the task is easier and the payoff is immeasurable.

Pay on your terms, but do it up-front. Remember, you will pay. Just pay up-front.

To ensure your success, you'll need a plan. I have been in professional coaching for years. I was introduced to the concept of life planning during coaching. Never heard of it until then. Then I halfheartedly accepted it. I didn't want to put the effort in. But after watching the successes of those who created and lived by life plans, I jumped in with both feet.

A life plan is critical to your success. It means you've spent true time uncovering what's been in your heart. Specifically your passion. That passion that you have, once uncovered, becomes a shining diamond that glows brightly before you always.

Your vision is created out of that passion. It becomes specific to you, your interests, and your talents. You find ways to couple your passion with your vision, using the skills and resources you've been given.

With your vision, you will need to identify how you want to live your life. Not just one element, but all the important elements. It's not enough to say you want to be successful. You have to define what success looks like to you. I'll share with you my life plan later, but I have ten critical areas I need to master if I'm going to view my life as a success. As I grow, some areas may drop off and other areas may hop on the list, but my success is clearly laid out for me.

You will have to understand your "why" too. Why is your passion important? Why is your vision important to achieve? Why is health important to you? Why is being a good parent important to you? What do you get out of it? Are the reasons you're focusing on that area compelling? If I say I want to lose twenty pounds, I need to identify why. For me, it's so I can live a long, healthy life and see my kids get involved with their kids. It's so I don't end up being fortunate to be in rehab because of heart issues. I want to run till I die. The reasons need to be compelling. For it to work, they need to emanate from your heart.

Steve Scanlon, president and CEO of Rewire, shared this with me:

> I wasn't quite considered "middle-aged" just yet. I was young, in my thirties, but still taking a long look down "middle age street." I had a great life with a decent job, four children. My life and my business by all counts were successful. The successes that I had experienced gave rise to indulgences that quickly led to a style of living that, among a host of other things, had me dangerously overweight and unhealthy.
>
> Upon waking one morning, I allowed my mind to tell myself that this weight gain had happened overnight and I could get rid of the issue just as easily. So I decided to lose weight by running a marathon. Forget the fact that I wasn't a runner nor had I ever run more than a mile in my life. I was fed up with my weight and I was "motivated." So why not start with a 26.2 mile marathon? It made perfect sense.
>
> With shoes in hand, I started my running campaign. Day one was a breeze. I went two miles and felt great. Day two? Check, and so on and so on ... for a week. Then when I hit the eighth or ninth day I remember negotiating within myself and losing. Same thing the following day. Each run was killed with an internal argument or excuse. Pretty soon I was off the plan and somewhat disgusted that I hadn't stuck to what I had committed to.
>
> I threw a pity party for myself. It lasted a few days. Then I decided that I'd force myself back to the task at hand.

On impulse, I entered into the Chicago Marathon and bought a plane ticket. I figured that money would be my motivator. A financial commitment would seal the deal. And it worked perfectly, for another week. Then the mental negotiations came back. I would lose those negotiations and end up with the same results.

Now I felt pathetic and was out the money that I used to force my commitment. I have a vague memory of coming up with some really healthy-sounding excuses so as to give myself a break from the beatings that my soul was taking. My body was fine, but my innermost soul was being pummeled. Deep down I just felt like a loser. It was bad.

Then I heard about the Leukemia and Lymphoma Society and how they had this internal program called Team in Training that provided a team, a coach, and if you raised money, they even paid your way to the marathon. At last there was a reprieve. I was in. I went to the training sessions and group runs. I met some great people and ran and ran. Then, after about ten days the mental negotiations returned and I was back on the couch. That was it. Done.

So I gave myself a plan that I could stick with. I'd quit. I just figured I could avoid the shame and pain by not making an effort. That was an easy goal and since I had already had disappointment, why bother with further disappointment. If I committed to quitting, I knew that I could hit that goal.

Soon, I was invited to a get-together of sorts put on by the Leukemia and Lymphoma team that I had abandoned.

I event was called a "patient honoree party." I didn't know anything about the party or what it entailed, but I would go just the same. At the party I met a girl named Katrina. Katrina was beautiful eight-year-old girl. She was completely hairless and stunning. I soon discovered that she had been in chemotherapy for five years. As we sat at the kitchen table of the event, I remember telling this sweet little eight year the woes of my life. "Life was hard for me," I told her. I was trying to run, but it was just too hard for me. My mind began to talk back to me. My ego-drenched mind failed for a moment as something down deep inside told me that I was telling this young girl, who only knew pain, how hard it was for me to run. "Can you imagine that?" my brain shot back. At some point she clued in on my emotional anguish and in an attempt to put me at ease, she reached across the table, clutched my arm and exclaimed "I have decided to make you my hero" (close your eyes and imagine you telling your problems to some eight year old chemo patient and having her reach across the table to reassure you). I was shell-shocked. I was not a Grinch, but into my life walked Little Cindy Lou to melt my heart just as she had the Grinch.

It is often said that the longest journey you will ever take is the eighteen inches from your head to your heart. That evening with Katrina, I made that trip, and like the Grinch, my heart grew many sizes that night. My heart became a rudder. Since then, my heart has grown so much that I have run fourteen marathons and have raised a lot of money for Leukemia and Lymphoma. A lot! In case you haven't figured out the moral of this story, I will put it plainly. Sustained action most often happens when our hearts our touched, not just our heads. It's imperative that your actions are born from your heart. Getting in shape, feeling healthier, setting goals are all good in and of themselves. But I tried and tried again until my heart had a purpose. When I found my purpose from within my heart, there would be nothing to stop me. Katrina passed away. But to this day I have some gifts that she gave me. I still run most every day. I am healthier and feel better, but what Katrina gave me, was the ability to let my heart take the lead in my life. Katrina lives with me and for that I will always be grateful.

Your plan need to be yours. It needs to come from your heart. After the plan comes accountability. With no accountability, your vision is only a dream. What are the steps you'll take to achieve each element of your life plan? For example, I want an awesome marriage with my wife. Marriage, as most people know, isn't easy. It takes work. Since I can't change others, I focus on the actions I can control. For example, to have a great marriage, I will need to invest in time with Michelle. One accountability item is for me to take her out to eat once a week, no kids. Maybe it's just breakfast. Maybe it's just lunch at a Subway. Maybe it's a fancy dinner, but since we have five kids, we can get so caught up with the family that we neglect spending time with each other. Since I want to model a good marriage for my kids, it's important they see me investing alone time with my wife. It needs to be on my calendar. Without that plan, my dream of a great marriage will be left to chance, a chance I don't want to take. Without the accountability, my marriage is left to happenstance.

There probably isn't a better life planning expert than Daniel Harkavy, the founder and president of Building Champions, a coaching company that helps people become all they're supposed to be. In Daniel's book on Life Planning that he cowrote with bestselling author Michael Hyatt goes through the entire life-planning process. Pick up the book to help you create your own life plan. It'll be the best investment you'll ever make in your personal life.

Building Champions has a "Building Champions Experience" annually. It's a couple of days dedicated to reviewing, updating, or creating life plans. Participants are limited in number, and it's held at a remote place to allow people like me to detach from Mach 1 lives and focus on what's important. One entire day is spent on my life plan.

After you create your life plan, you'll read it daily for about two weeks, then weekly for the next two or three months, then monthly to make sure your actions are in line with your life plan.

The life plan begins with a eulogy. What do you want people to say about you at your funeral? What you want them to say at your funeral may be very different than what they would say about you today. That's okay. Create your eulogy the way you hope others will think of you when you die.

In the interest of transparency, I share my eulogy and my life plan with you. Don't laugh at my eulogy. Well, okay, laugh, but it's what I hope people will say about me when I die. "Hope" is the operative word here. I hope that's what they will say. My life plan isn't your life plan. Yours My life plan isn't your life plan. Yours may look similar, but it very well may be markedly different.

Eulogy: What will people say about your life?

Larry lived a long fulfilling life with his wife, Michelle. He is survived by his five children, Brett, Jake, Claire, Grant, and Tessa. He was a loving husband and father. Although brilliantly financially successful, Larry's passions surrounded his family and positively impacted the lives of those with whom he came in contact. He ran a successful region for a national mortgage company, but during that time, he found that his passions impacted people's lives.

He spent most all his free time with Michelle and their children. After years of success at Cherry Creek Mortgage, he felt a passion to write a book. His first book, *No Rewind*, spent weeks at the top of the *New York Times* best seller list.

Although involved with charities, the success of *No Rewind* allowed him to invest even more heavily in charities, particularly those in ministries and those revolving around kids and teens. After *No Rewind*, he became a sought-after speaker. He wrote many more bestselling books.

He took care of his health and loved spending free time in the Arctic with his dad and brothers. He spent a lot of time with his family fishing and mountain climbing.

All of his children have followed in his legacy and are successful in their own rights.

LARRY BETTAG'S LIFE PLAN

My life plan isn't rocket science. Those who read it may think I'm a braggart. I haven't done a lot of what I've written in my life plan, but I hope to before I die, and I hope my future successes will be talked about at my funeral. Your life plan is personal to you. You needn't share it with anyone. In my hopes of impacting your life, I'm sharing mine with you. I hope it gives you an example as to format and maybe a few ideas.

My life is a gift from God, and I'm entitled to His protection as I live in Him. As Christ gave His life for me, I, too, give my life to Him. I am here on earth to shine as a beacon to those in the dark. I am to lead the way He instructs me to lead. I am to follow Him always. The candle that has been given to me shall always shine and never be placed under a basket.

I live assured that my wife, my children, and I partake as heirs to the kingdom and receive eternal life. I live life on purpose, looking to accomplish the goals below. My purpose is to leave a lasting legacy that will carry on after I join Christ in heaven. I will become a bestselling author who impacts lives even after I leave this earth.

I. I will value my life with Christ*

Jesus Christ died on the cross for me. He was employed by His father to set me free. I value and embrace that gift. Likewise, I am employed by Christ

---

* I know ... pretty cliché, but true, and it's what I aspire to.

to glorify Him. I lust after Christ with the passion someone in a desert craves water. I seek to be less so that He is more. I develop my relationship with Christ and utilize the talents He has entrusted me with.

I don't let my past sins and failings determine my mood or take me away from my purpose. If I were perfect, I'd be Christ or I'd be in heaven. My past shortcomings do not dictate my future.

Action Plan

- spend time daily in God's Word, reading for no less than five minutes a day, asking for His counsel
- pray daily
- have weekly devotional time apart from the chaos of life to worship, praise, reflect on, and petition God

These three actions are non-negotiable.

II. I value my wife, Michelle

"They are no longer two, but one. Whatever God has joined together, let no man separate." Matthew 19:6 NEW INTERNATIONAL VERSION Love your wife as Christ so loved the church. I value Michelle and spend time daily praising, loving, encouraging, and leading her. I lend a hand and support her in her personal, physical, mental, and spiritual development. My actions with Michelle are actions that unite us, not divide us. Divorce is not acceptable to Christ, Michelle, or me. We pray together and converse to build each other up.

I spend weekly time with her that is set apart intentionally and away from the busy life work and family demand. I invest my time in her so I can be even more in love with her than I was when we were dating. The bottom line is that I invest time in her and our relationship so we grow together. We love each other a lot, but not nearly as much as we will in the future. Specific time investments will be made by me weekly to connect, support, and understand her.

Action Plan

- help her around the house and with the children the minute I walk through the door
- give her weekly affirmations about how much I love and appreciate her
- take her out for alone time at least once a week for lunch, dinner, or a date
- have two getaways a year with just her

III. I value my children

Brett, Jake, Claire, Grant, and Tessa were created by Christ and entrusted to me. He has a predetermined purpose for each of them, and it's my job to help them achieve it. There is no greater gift to a child than providing him or her with siblings. My wife and I have a purpose of raising modern-day kings and queens to be heirs of the kingdom. Leaders of the kingdom. To duplicate and leverage the DNA gifts God has provided each child.

It is my duty to love, nurture, and pray for them and their vocations and any prospective spouses God may have for them. I am to recognize, develop, and nurture the gifts God has placed in each one. I will lead through prayer and by example. By my time invested into them, they will know for certain I love them unconditionally.

Action Plan

- spend weekly time alone with each of them
- praise, encourage, love, and discipline them so they will make their marks on the world and their future families
- have one-on-one days with each of them once a quarter

- continue family nights, during which one kid picks out the menu, we shop together, we prep the food together, and we cook together (I will do this weekly for at least 70 percent of each year.)
- pray with each of them when tucking them in bed and let them know I'm so excited God put them in my life

IV. I value my siblings, parents, and extended family

I have been blessed with parents who love me. They pray and care for me. Although it's my desire that my parents spend more time with us and with their grandchildren, I cannot force them to do so. I respect the fact they have four other sons and daughters and can spend only a limited time with me and my family.

My parents have taught me loyalty and faithfulness. Through their example, I am loving and faithful to them as well. I am to lead an exemplary life and use the gifts God has given me to make my parents proud. I love my siblings and have been blessed to have been raised with the best siblings ever. I value them and know because of time and geography, my physical interaction with them will be limited. I will invest time each year in furthering my relationships with my siblings.

Action Plan

- call each sibling at least once a month to catch up
- get together with each one at least once a year
- see my parents monthly, inviting them for dinner

V. I value my health

This is my biggest struggle. I'm healthy. I've lost weight this past year, but I need to do more. My body is a temple of the Holy Spirit, and I will treat it that way. Without treating my body as such, I cannot do any of the things in my life plan. I eat proper foods in proper amounts. I exercise and "keep the flesh under." I am in control of my body and submit it to me and Christ. I value my health, don't take it for granted, and do my best to protect it. I need to make sure I get a proper amount of sleep.

Action Plan

- cut down on alcohol (Although I don't drink much, having two beers on weekend nights needs to be trimmed to perhaps once or twice a month.)
- cut down on food intake Monday through Friday, and make sure it's healthy food—and measured
- temper my love for food with my desire for a healthier lifestyle
- continue to work out—four times a week minimum, five times a week ideal

VI. I value the country I live in and its religious freedom

I cannot believe God selected me to be born in the blessings of the United States rather than the sickness of Africa, the ignorance of the Middle East, or the poverty and loneliness of the Ukraine. I must realize I have been spoiled by God thereby. I cannot get caught up with the gifts God has given me but be blind to Him. I need to use those freedoms to support keeping those freedoms and fight diligently to support those whose job it is to keep those freedoms alive.

Action Plan

- support the tenets of the constitution
- invest in organizations that protect the constitution
- vote each election
- support candidates who support the constitution

VII. I value my church

I love St. Patrick's Church. I love the education I was provided. I love the fact I can provide the same for my children.

Action Plan

- tithe from my income
- attend Mass at least once per week besides Sundays
- attend weekly adoration of Christ
- support the Christian Church and live by its tenets

VIII. I use the talents God gave me

People tell me I'm a good writer. I like to influence others. I need to stay on task and focused on utilizing the skills God has given me.

Action Plan

- spend five hours a week finishing my book
- begin my second book as soon as the first goes to print

IX. I value humility

While I may be confident, I am not arrogant. I strive to know I am employed by my boss, Jesus Christ. I do my best to listen to His voice, seek His counsel, and know His Word. I enjoy the fact I can learn from others. Others have DNA and gifts I do not or ever will possess.

God took mercy on me; I am always mindful of the fact that it was not me who made me the success I am today. This humility remains the core of my growth and my being. This humility helped land me where I am today. The humility stays. It's imperative for my continued growth and success.

I don't have a heart that rebels against God or others who are not like me. I learn from both. In all my ways, I acknowledge Him.

My Mission

My mission is to seek first the kingdom of God and His righteousness. I recognize that I have failed miserably in this area but that God has given me a fresh start. I seize the moment. I identify my gaps in life and seek remedies for them. I play to win. For me to be the best, to become the person God created me to be, I must do everything to win. I will conquer. I do all things through Christ who strengthens me.

"I have fought the good fight, I have finished the race, I have kept the faith" (2 Timothy 4:7). NEW INTERNATIONAL VERSION

AFTERWORD: KEEPING YOUR FUSE LIT

Now what? You've read the stories. Your heart has been spoken to. Can you commit to yourself and your dream? Of course you can. It's time. You're reading this book for a reason, and the best part about it is that it doesn't concern me or anyone else. It's all about you and God. Sure, others are woven into your dreams, but your dreams are all yours. If your heart is stirring, I'm thrilled. It's all about you anyway. It has to be. It's your passion, not mine. What's your commitment to yourself?

1. **Wendy—The Desire for Something Better:** You don't need a crappy life to want something better. You don't need a crappy life to have a dream. The fact Wendy had such horrible parents made her passion all that more clear to her. It was obvious to Wendy what she needed to do to fulfill her dreams. You probably haven't been violated as Wendy had been, but most likely, you're working with some unfulfilled dreams. Your homework? Rediscover your dream. Pull it out. Dust it off. Find your calling. Start taking the steps necessary to achieve it.

2. **Faith—No One Walks Alone:** Well, at least no truly happy person walks alone. I believe there's a God. I want His protection, leadership, and wisdom. You may have walked away from God. You may believe God doesn't exist (He does), but since this book isn't about me proving I'm right or you proving you're right,

this is a simple question between you and God. Do you honestly believe? Do you want help in achieving your goals and dreams? It starts with true transparency between you and the Father. Even though I'm an attorney, when you die, I won't be there with you before God to argue your case. Nor will you be there when I die to argue my case. So I'm irrelevant to you and your walk with God as you are with mine. But find a place by yourself. Perhaps it's the corner spot in the parking lot away from everyone else or the closet in the bedroom when everyone else has left the house, but get real with God. It starts with your true seeking of Him and your true transparency. Starting today, you will have an honest and transparent relationship with your Father. You just might hear, "Ahhh, Grasshoppa."

3. **David—Yesterday Is Gone:** Those mistakes. Those sins. The faults. You know them. Your friends tell you about them. When you lay your head on the pillow, the voices come. *You suck. You'll never amount to anything.* Your past is your past. It doesn't matter except to learn from. At that point, you let go of the past. You don't bury it. You let it go. If your past truly defined you, your life might as well be over, but you know the past doesn't define you. Like David, you hold your head up high and start moving toward your mission. You ask God for forgiveness, but more important, you forgive yourself. You can't walk forward when you are always looking back. Your past is just that. It's your past, and for the first time in your life, it will remain in your past since you will no longer carry it. You have moved on to fulfill your calling.

4. **Fear of Change:** Everything in life is in a state of decay. Leave a car in the garage for two years without starting it and it will fall apart. You grow or you die. You will have pain. But you choose the pain. Change involves pain. It also involves the fear of the unknown. Few people "get off" on change, but some do. With change, there very well may be many things unknown to you.

But consider the alternative—keeping things easy, the status quo. The pain this choice carries is the lack of dreams fulfilled. You, however, have chosen the former. You rise to the challenge. You see the goal before you, a mountain you are climbing. There may be times when you reach a ridge thinking you've summited only to see the real peak still far away, but you continue. You've made the commitment. You're on that mountain, and there's no turning back. You've been given your talents. Use them. You refuse to die with the word *potential* attached to your name.

5. **Putting Faith to Work:** There comes a time when you have nothing to rely on other than faith. Not faith and hope. Just faith. Your faith will be tested. Can you stand? Will you stand? When others say your dream is futile or hopeless, or when you can't see a way for your project to succeed, you will stand strong. You know your vision has been placed in your heart. You know you need to keep driving forward. You will do it because you know your calling. *Where there's a will there's a way*, you tell yourself. You have your rock Scriptures. You have your rock reminders. When all else falls away, two things remain: your vision and your dream, and you won't relinquish them.

6. **Michael—Passion:** Passion drove Michael Jordan to make the team and become the best of all time. Your passion needs to remain. Your passion needs to be fueled. You will feed your passion. You have spent time discovering your passion. It's brand new and shiny. It's not buried anymore. Your passion will never be buried again. Just like Michael, defeat serves only to help you become more determined in your quest for greatness. Each failure is an opportunity for you to learn, grow, and become better at your craft. Your passion remains.

7. **Eric—Persistence:** Eric knew if he was to achieve his goals, quitting was not an option. Persistence, diligence, and single-minded

purpose were his only options. You have the option to not be single minded. The work may be too hard for you. You can't see the grueling effort it would take for you to achieve your goals. But as Eric learned when the patient came into his room and told him life was good with the status quo, you too refuse to accept the status quo. You will outwork your competition. You will work harder than everyone else. No one works with a single-minded purpose more than you do. Opportunities that don't align with your vision are distracters. Good is the enemy of great. Your refusal to quit will take you where you need to go. You will break your goal down into discrete steps. Upon taking each step, you will hear your bell ring. You will define your bell, and you will hear it ring.

8. **Josette—Love:** You can have the faith to move mountains, but without love, it's meaningless. You can win the war and lose the battle. Someone recently asked me to contribute money to a girl who needed money for a new heart. I passed on the offer. I was already fully invested in five charities. But all week I couldn't let it go. I was invested in those charities because of love, but in being narrow minded in my focus, I lost the mission of love. I made a contribution happily after I did my gut check. You too will walk in love. Love is not a feeling. Sure, you can have great feelings with love, but love is expressed in action. You will show the world you love from your heart. Like the Grinch, your heart will grow ten times its normal size because you have made the choice to love. Love is supreme. Love changes your heart, and it'll open the heavens to rain down on you. You will choose to love. You will make the effort, and you will receive so much more than you could ever give.

9. **Life Planning:** You have learned so much. Now you are taking charge of your life. You will write down the most important things in your life. It will become your bible. You will be true to

the most important things in your life. You won't let anything interfere with your passions. You'll set aside time to create your plan. You'll read it daily in the beginning and then weekly and monthly later. You'll discover you have bigger passions that replace some of the passions you started with. You'll amend the life plan as you grow and begin to experience success.

Many people think success comes down to rocket science. It doesn't. It comes down to a decision. A decision from the heart. It's my hope that you make your decision for greatness. Your successes and failures of yesterday are yesterday's. Use them to learn and grow from, but don't let them define you. You have so much of your life still to live. Make each day count.

The formula is really easy. First, recognize what your talents are. You have something special you were designed to excel at. Throw away all humility for a moment and discover what that is. Then build your life plan. Read Daniel Harkavy and Michael Hyatt's book, They have mastered the life planning process.

Know that there are no rewinds. What you do tomorrow and the next day can't be undone. If you fail, get over it and get back up. What are the things that excite your soul? You have the ability to impact the world.

Stop living for momentary pleasure. Trade it for eternal fulfillment. Use your life to impact the lives of others. Do what you do and ask God to open the doors that need to be opened and to shut the doors that need to be shut. It is only then that you will begin to find your path.

I heard the great motivational speaker, Andy Andrews, tell a story about Joshua Chamberlain, a schoolteacher who became a very critical player in the Civil War. He was with the North, on a hill, trying to hold his position against the South. They ran out of ammunition. Every time they repelled the South, they would scavenge the bodies for ammunition. When they finally ran out of even this source for ammunition, he told his troops they would charge the South with everything they had. They were successful, and he became a hero in the north.

What is interesting is that the South had a sniper up in a tree, ready to take down Chamberlain. After the war was over, the sniper sought out Josh. I forget if he met him in person or sent him a letter, but his communication astonished me. He said the fighting had been brisk. The valley was filled with gunpowder smoke. Every once in a while, the smoke would clear, and the sniper would get a clear view of Josh in his gun sight. For whatever reason, the sniper, who had killed many before Josh, said he just wasn't able to pull the trigger on Joshua. He tried and tried but couldn't bring himself to pull the trigger on Joshua.

Andy's message was clear to me and those in the audience. So long as you're doing what God has called you to do, you can't be taken until your mission is complete. He's called you to do something great. Something awesome.

Discover what your mission is. Own it. The impact you will make may change the lives of just one person or it may forever change the direction of the world. Find yours. Own yours.

CAN I ASK A FAVOR OF YOU?

It's my prayer and hope that this book would actually inspire you. It's my desire that through reading this book that you would take action to improve your life, to reach for your goals, or in the very least make positive changes in your life which will significantly improve the quality of your life.

If you have found this book to be of any benefit to you, can I ask a favor of you? Can you talk about this to someone? Can you recommend it on Amazon or on Facebook? Can you write a blog about it if you enjoyed it? Can you buy a copy for a friend who needs some help or for a friend who loves reading great books (I hope that this book will qualify). I would have to believe that you wouldn't get this far in the book unless you found some value in it.

People don't receive without asking, so I'm asking. Please help to spread the word. That's my one favor. I want to continue this journey, but the word needs to spread. I want this message out there, so I'll need your help.

So, in advance, I say thank you for anything you've done to support this book, my mission and this message. I'm humbled that you read the book and am grateful for anything that you would do to promote the book. Thank you!

ACKNOWLEDGMENTS

Although it's so chic to thank Christ, I thank Him as my real Lord and Savior. He is patient, forgiving, encouraging, and endearing to the biggest meathead to have ever walked the face of earth. I don't know why He didn't take me when He could have. For whatever reasons, God saw greater things in me than even I saw in myself. He refused to let go of my potential even when I didn't know there was a plan for me. "Ahhh, Grasshoppa," He still says to me today.

I thank my wife, Michelle. Not too long ago, we looked at each other with blinding twinkles in our eyes. That led to marriage, five kids, and chaos. Zoinks! You're probably the hardest-working woman I have ever met. You work hard for the family and have always believed I would do something great. If being married to me and 5.5 kids doesn't make you a little loopy, I don't know what will. You have to have a few loose screws yourself to be married to me, but I'm so grateful. God did well when He put you in my life. Thank you, Michelle! I love you Michelle.

Brett, Jake, Claire, Grant, and Tessa, you rock my world. I'm the biggest kid, I know, and you remind me of that every day. Fortunately, God has created this ridiculous desire in me to love, take care of, and protect you. To that extent, God has really forced me to grow up a bit. I pray I do as good a job raising you as you are doing raising me. I love you all.

Mom and Dad, I want to cry as I write this, but I can never put into words the impact you've had on my life. A great marriage is set by example. I try to love Michelle and be a good father and husband because of you two. You were the best examples, and I'm afraid you were better parents to me than I am to my kids, but I'm still just learning. I'm glad you're still here on earth so I can seek your wisdom. Thank you for your love and prayers.

Mark, Linda, Eric, and Matt, you are the best siblings any brother could ask for. I used to get so mad that each of you got married because it took away time we could spend with each other. Then I screwed everything up by getting married myself. I get it. I wouldn't be as fun or as crazy without you. Thanks for putting up with my antics over the years. You were the best audience any showoff could have asked for.

Jessi, you blessed my life when you were with us. I can't wait to see what you and God will accomplish in your future.

Jeff and Stacey, you guys are the best. Thanks for not giving up on me. We have the same passions, core values, and interests. I'm blessed to have worked for you. Thank you. Words can never express the gratitude I have for you both.

Josette, you are my love. You are the love of my family. You are an inspiration to me constantly. I can't wait for us to work together. I'm convinced we will have a day together. Go Irish. My prayers are with you always, my friend. Here's to the rest of your story. Just sitting on the sidelines, I feel blessed to be connected to you.

Jim, thanks for being my friend. Thanks for letting me rattle your cage since fifth grade. I have been paying you back forever ever since that Z push. You are everything that I am not. Thank you.

Joyce, thank you for your friendship over the years. You're not a business associate but a great friend, and for that I'm grateful. It's been a long time together, hasn't it? Thanks for always pushing me. You do it well! Keep pushing too. I need it.

Joe, I know you're looking down on me from heaven. I think of you always. You are my brotha from anotha motha! I pray for my goddaughter daily. I think you may have been sent to heaven to look after your goddaughter. You're gone, but you've never left.